Marriage Melodious

♥♥♥

By
Pastor D. A. Waite, Th.D., Ph.D.

the
**BIBLE
FOR
TODAY**
900 Park Avenue
Collingswood, NJ 08108
Phone: 856-854-4452
www.BibleForToday.org

BFT #3006

Published by

**The Bible For Today Press
900 Park Avenue
Collingswood, New Jersey 08108
U.S.A.
856-854-4452**

January, 2003

BFT #3006

Copyright, 2003
All Rights Reserved

ISBN #1-56848-033-4

Table of Contents

Acknowledgments viii
Foreword ix
Introductory Comments 1
    A. Some Analogies Between Music and Marriage 1
    B. My Qualifications to Speak on Marriage 3
    C. The Bible Is Our Manual and our Map for a
        "melodious marriage" 4
    D. The Outline of the Material 4

Chapter One
The Maker of a Melodious Marriage 5

    A. A Summary (Genesis 1) 5
        1. The Source 5
        2. The Stamp 5
        3. The Separateness 6
        4. The Splendor 7
        5. The Supplication 7
    B. A Synthesis (Genesis 2) 7
        1. The Substance 7
        2. The Soul 8
        3. The Service 8
        4. The Selectivity 9
        5. The Solitude 9
        6. The Solution 10
        7. The Surgery 10
        8. The Solemnizing 10
        9. The Strategy 11
    C. A Shame (Genesis 3) 12
        1. The Susceptibility 12
        2. The Sin 12
        3. The Shame 13
        4. The Shifting 13

5. The Sentence 14
6. The Succession 14
7. The Sacrifice 15
8. The Servitude 16
9. Summary 17

Chapter Two
The Managers of a Melodious Marriage 19

A. The Duties of Christian Wives to Christian Husbands 19
   1. The Submission 19
   2. The Subordination 25
   3. The Severity 26

B. The Duties of Christian Husbands to Christian Wives 26
   1. The Superintendency 27
   2. The Sacrifice 27
   3. The Sanctification 28
   4. The Selfishness 28
   5. The Separation 29
   6. The Sticking 29
   7. The Sexuality 31
   8. The Sensibility 31
   9. The Sample 33

Chapter 3
The Mutuality of a Melodious Marriage 37

A. The Sexuality 39
B. The Supplications 53
C. The Sensitivity 54
D. The Steadfastness 54
E. Other Sentiments 55

Table of Contents

Chapter 4
The Multiplication of a Melodious Marriage 59

- **A. Parents' Duties Regarding their Children** 60
  1. The Stress 60
  2. The Supervision 62
  3. The Spanking 63
  4. The Speaking 64
  5. The Sparing 65
  6. The Spoiling 66
  7. The Stupidity 66
  8. The Salvation 67
  9. The Shame 67
  10. The Serenity 68
- **B. Examples of Bringing Up Children in the Bible** 69
  1. Sad Examples of Bringing up Children 69
     a. The Slaying--Eli's Sons 69
     b. The Sinning--Samuel's Sons 71
  2. Good Examples of Bringing up Children 71
     a. The Serving--Ruth 71
     b. The Searching--Joshua & Caleb 72
     c. The Steadfastness--Daniel 73
     d. The Standing--Shadrach, Meshach & Abednego ... 75
- **C.** Other Thoughts For Helping Our Children 76

Conclusions 78
Index of Words and Phrases 81
About the Author 93
Order Blank Pages 95

Acknowledgments

I wish to acknowledge the assistance of the following people:

● **The Congregation** of the Bible For Today Baptist Church whose gifts made possible the printing and publication of this study by their Pastor;

● **Yvonne Sanborn Waite**, my wife, who encouraged the publication of this series, read the manuscript several times, and gave helpful suggestions;

● **Dianne W. Cosby**, for typing these messages from the cassette tapes and putting them in computer format;

● **Daniel S. Waite**, the Assistant to the Bible For Today Director, who guided the book through the printing process;

● **Barbara Egan**, our Bible For Today secretary who also read the manuscript and offered valuable comments.

Foreword

♥♥♥

Foreword

By: Pastor D. A. Waite, Th.D., Ph.D.
Bible For Today Baptist Church
900 Park Avenue, Collingswood, NJ 08108
Phone: 856-854-4452; FAX: 856-854-2464;
E-mail: BFT@BibleForToday.org;
Website: www.BibleForToday.org

First Person. Excuse me if I write this booklet in the first person, just as I preached and taught it. It is not written as a usual book might be written. Instead, it is in outline form with a few comments under each of the points. This is the outline that I used when I spoke at a three-day married couples retreat at a camp in Ohio in 1987. My daughter typed the words as I said them using the outline as I taught it.

Important Subject. Marriage is a very important subject, and I do not mean to de-emphasize its importance by using this outline format. I hope that, in this form, it might still have a vital impact on the couples and soon-to-be couples who read it. I have used alliteration throughout, as you can see. I have also used the numbers and letters normally used in an outline in order to keep the topics in their proper order of emphasis.

Tapes. The original messages are available as **BFT #1454/1-4** for a gift of **$12.00 plus $4.00** shipping and handling. It is hoped that this book might be used of the Lord Jesus Christ to strengthen our Christian homes in a successful attempt at **MAKING MARRIAGE MELODIOUS**.

Some Important Verses on Marriage

"**Whoso findeth a wife findeth a good _thing_**, and obtaineth favour of the LORD." (Proverbs 18:22)

"Let thy fountain be blessed: and **rejoice with the wife of thy youth**." (Proverbs 5:18)

"House and riches _are_ the inheritance of fathers: and **a prudent wife _is_ from the LORD**." (Proverbs 19:14)

Introductory Comments

In many ways, marriage is like music. The husband and wife are like musicians. God is the Composer of the music of marriage. He has committed us to a lifetime of practice together.

A. Some Analogies Between Music and Marriage

1. **God Himself is the COMPOSER of MELODIOUS MARRIAGE.** He has committed married people to a lifetime of practice together with one husband and one wife until death parts them. He is the Composer--the One who sets forth the principles of how to make a marriage melodious. We must realize this.

2. **We must know the SCORE of God's composition.** In musical terms, a "score" is *"a printed copy of music which shows all the parts for the instruments or voices."* We must know how God wrote the marriage score.

3. **We must WANT to follow that SCORE.** We must want to follow God's way in our marriage, not our own way.

4. **We must ACTUALLY FOLLOW that SCORE.** It is more than just a "want to," we must actually follow that score.

5. **BOTH husband and wife must perform their PARTS as written in the SCORE.** If this is not done, there is nothing but empty confusion and dissonance.

6. **Marriage begins as a DUET, NOT a SOLO.** In marriage, there are two of us. When we are joined in marriage our solo life is history. When children come, marriage becomes a trio, quartet, quintet, sextet, etc.--an **ORCHESTRA!**

7. The MUSIC can be a HARMONY or a CACOPHONY. It might be a terrible din of confusion. It's up to the musicians.
8. MELODY must be easily discernable, NOT like a very elaborate special piano solo where it is <u>**DISGUISED**</u>. This discernable melody is the kind of music like the hymn, "Jesus Keep Me Near the Cross." On the other hand, you have composers like Beethoven who interweave many other musical notes in their music and, at times, disguise the melody. In a "melodious marriage" the melody must be easily discernable to all those who look upon it, and especially to our mates.
9. Some days MARRIAGE is NOT IN GOOD VOICE. Our INSTRUMENTS are not warmed up. They may be COLD, thus making them FLAT or SHARP. In case you know anything about musical instruments, let me explain. For instance, if the brass instrument is cold it is a little sharp.
10. Some days the MARRIAGE has LARYNGITIS. We are not able to speak to each other as well as we should.
11. Some days MARRIAGE is OFF-KEY, OUT OF HARMONY, and on the WRONG BEAT.
12. To make MELODIOUS MELODY, we must do a lot of PRACTICING. I noticed some of you have been "practicing" in your marriages for 40 years. I've been practicing over 54 years as of this writing. Some couples only have one year of practice. Marriage takes a lot of **faithful** and **steady** practicing to make it harmonious.
13. Do YOU really want a MELODIOUS MARRIAGE? It takes TWO. Both husband and wife really must want a "melodious marriage."
14. There are NO MARRIAGES in Heaven. This is your ONLY chance--NOW! You can make it melodious or you can make it cacophonous.
15. In some MARRIAGES, there is a LOST CHORD. There is something missing. It's up to the couples to find the harmony.
16. Practicing the SCALES is fundamental in making MELO-DIOUS MUSIC. I know, when I took piano, playing the scales were a major part of my practice. I took concert clarinet and scales were part of my practice there as well. I had to get that fingering

down just right. It was the same with the saxophone. It is the same with marriage. The marriage fundamentals are like musical scales.

17. **MARRIAGE MELODY does NOT use a SOUND TRACK. It is always LIVE MUSICAL ACCOMPANIMENT.** There should be nothing artificial or "canned" in a "melodious marriage."

18. **No one is BORN with the ability to PLAY AN INSTRUMENT perfectly.** It takes PRACTICE. So with marriage. You are not born that way. You have to learn. Whether it is the piano, the flute, the harp, or any other instrument. You have to learn to play. The same is true with marriage.

19. **MELODY can be made with only ONE person.** If your spouse is out of melody you can make melody in the house anyway.

20. **HARMONY requires TWO or more persons.** You cannot make harmony by yourself, only melody. Harmony takes two.

21. **RHYTHM is doing the RIGHT thing at the RIGHT TIME.** If you get off-beat and off-rhythm that is not good for music or for a marriage.

B. My Qualifications to Speak on Marriage.

1. <u>I Have Been Married since 1948 ; Four Sons, One Daughter; Four Married Children; Eight Grandchildren (Three Boys & Five Girls)</u>. Mrs. Waite and I have observed our own marriage during these many years. It is impossible not to have had some difficult times in fifty-four years of marriage. We have lived through them. There have been arguments with the children and with each other just like in other families. We have found the answer to many of these pitfalls after our years together and are still looking for answers in some cases. With the Lord's help He has enabled us to stick together. We want to keep it that way. We trust that you do as well.

2. <u>I Was a Naval Chaplain, Five Years on Active Duty (1956–1961)</u>, with about 3,000 to 4,000 cases of all kinds in counseling situations. I don't often speak on this theme, only when I am asked. I was asked in Illinois last summer and I spoke on it. In our country, there are many conferences on the family. Sometimes it seems that those who speak the loudest on "Marriage and Family" are the first to fall into adultery, fornication, and the breaking-up of their own homes. I do not want this to happen to me because I am speaking on this theme.

You watch and look at some of those involved in marriage ministry. There was a woman who spoke for years on "Marriage and the Home"; yet later, she became divorced. One of my former pastors spoke all the time on the family. Yet, his own home was destroyed by his own foolishness. He committed adultery with a woman in his church for a period of about two years. He was an "expert" on the family.

C. The Bible Is Our Manual and our Map for a Melodious Marriage.

Let us look into the Word of God together. We are going to see from the Scriptures what God has for us in a *"melodious marriage."*

D. The OUTLINE of the Book:

The outline that I will follow is simple:
1. "The **MAKER** of a Melodious Marriage."
2. "The **MANAGERS** of a Melodious Marriage."
3. "The **MUTUALITY** of a Melodious Marriage."
4. "The **MULTIPLICATION** of a Melodious Marriage."

Chapter One
The Maker of a Melodious Marriage

The first thing I want to consider is "The **MAKER** of a Melodious Marriage." It is taken from Genesis Chapters 1-3. If you have your Bible you might want to turn to Genesis Chapter I. We need at the very outset to take a look at the **FOUNDATIONS of MARRIAGE** in the Word of God.

A. A Summary (Genesis 1). Because there are a number of points to touch, I will be able to spend only a brief time on each. These points are very simple. They are neither deep nor profound. First of all I want you to see a summary of God's creation as found in Genesis, Chapter 1.

- **1. THE SOURCE.**

Genesis 1:26a: *"And GOD said, Let US MAKE man . . ."* The source of all marriage is God Himself.

> a. Man was CREATED by a personal God.
> b. Man was NOT EVOLVED.

To understand the Maker of marriage, we must realize that the Maker of marriage created us. Any couples who do not have that fact firmly placed in mind have their marriages headed for the rocks. Whether the marriage is for Christian couples or unsaved couples, God Himself is the Source of a melodious and harmonious marriage.

- **2. THE STAMP.**

(1:26b): *". . . IN OUR IMAGE, after our LIKENESS:"*
(1:27a) *"So God CREATED MAN IN HIS OWN IMAGE, in the IMAGE OF GOD CREATED HE HIM"*

> a. **Man was made in God's IMAGE.**

Man has a spirit, a soul, and a body. He has three parts. He is tripartite. That image is like the tripartite nature of God (Father, Son, and Holy Spirit). Paul mentions our tripartite nature in 1 Thessalonians chapter 5:23: *". . . I pray God your whole spirit, and soul, and body be preserved blameless. . ."* The stamp of the Divine image on us is that we have intellect that corresponds to our spirit; we have sensibility or feelings that correspond to our soul; and we have will that corresponds to our body. We are persons, and we have personalities. God stamped us with His Divine image. We are not animals. *"In the image of God,"* God made man.

● **3. THE SEPARATENESS.**

(1:27b): *". . . MALE and FEMALE created He them."* He made males separate from females. The women liberationists say that there is not any difference between male and female. They say that if you teach a boy how to play with a doll, he will play with it just like a girl plays with it. That's false. *"Male and female created he them."* God made us different.

> a. This "MALE & FEMALE," precludes unisex and every form of homosexuality.

God Is Against Homosexuality. God made men to be men and women to be women! We must oppose vigorously this unisex push, including the unisex hair styles, and all the philosophy that goes with it. Unisexual thinking leads to homosexual thinking. That's the false thinking of the so-called Gay Rights Movement. That movement teaches that we are all basically the same and that there is little difference between males and females. "Androgyny" is the word that Virginia Mollenkott (the self-admitted "Christian" lesbian) uses to refer to humanity. This word comes from two Greek words, "ANER" (male) and "GYNE" (female). She says that men and women are androgynous. Androgyny means that everybody is half man and half woman. She even teaches that the Lord Jesus Christ was androgynous, that is, He was both a man and a woman. This is as blasphemous as it is untrue!

Lesbian Mollenkott Backs This Sin. Mrs. Mollenkott tries to confuse this matter in order to justify her female homosexuality. She has written a book called, *Women, Men, and the Bible*. Virginia Mollenkott used to teach at Shelton College. I taught part time on the Ringwood, NJ Campus of Shelton

Chapter One—The Maker of a Melodious Marriage

College when she taught there. She was married at the time and had a son. She divorced her husband and has been living a lesbian lifestyle with various women ever since.

- **4. THE SPLENDOR.**
    (1:28a): *"And God BLESSED THEM . . ."*

> a. God blessed Adam and Eve.

I believe that they realized God's blessings on them. This is indeed splendor when God blesses a home and the couple understands His blessings upon them and thanks Him for it.

- **5. THE SUPPLICATION.**
    1:28b): *". . BE FRUITFUL and MULTIPLY, and REPLENISH THE EARTH, . . ."*

> a. God commanded Adam and Eve to "be fruitful."

There was no thought of murdering children by means of abortions. They were to love children, even before pets or other animals. Maybe you are not able to have children. The Lord knows all about that. One brother said he had some spiritual children, and that's fine. Some who are unable to have children of their own have showed their love for children by adopting them. Often the adopted children are loved as much as if they were their very own. In view of God's love for children, it is indeed sad that there are 1.5 million abortions per year in the United States alone.

B. A Synthesis (Genesis 2).

- **1. THE SUBSTANCE.**
    (2:7a) : *"And the Lord formed man of the DUST of the ground."* There are not two creation stories here. There are not two creations. In Genesis 1:26, we see the overall picture. In Genesis Chapter 2, we see the details. We ought not to say that these are two separate stories and conflicting accounts. Let's take a look at some of the things we find in Genesis Chapter 2 concerning the foundation of marriage and God the Maker of marriage.

> a. *"dust of the ground."*

God Opposes Evolution. There is no evolution here, either atheistic or theistic. *"Dust"* is the substance of our being. You and I who are married should realize that we are but dust. Dr. Erwin Moon of Moody Bible Institute, years ago, had a film out called, "Dust or Destiny." Maybe some of you Moody graduates remember that. It was a good and interesting film. We are made of dust, but we also have a glorious destiny if we are a born again believer.

Dust to Dust. At death, the body decays and goes back to dust from which it was taken. The value, as far as the chemicals and different materials and minerals, is very small. The value used to be a few cents. Now it is a dollar and so many cents because of inflation. We cannot expect of dust something other than what we have. That's why, *"All have sinned and come short of the glory of God."* The word for dust is "APHAR" in the Hebrew Text. This dust was inanimate (lifeless) dust, not animate (alive). The Bible does not teach evolution in any form, either theistic evolution or natural evolution. The Bible teaches special creation.

Ockenga's Sub-Man Theory. I remember Dr. Harold John Ockenga, the father of Neo-Evangelicalism. When I was the pastor of Faith Baptist Church in Newton, Massachusetts, he was pastoring close by in Boston's Park Street Church. He wrote the book, *Women and the Bible*. He mentioned that the dust of Genesis was animate. He believed in the "sub-man" theory. This theory holds that man evolved into a kind of a sub-man or beast with two legs. This is theistic evolution. Ockenga said that all God did was to breathe into that "sub-man" to give it life. That is how he explained creation. This is just false and unscriptural. The Lord formed man out of the inanimate dust of the ground. There was no life at all in that dust.

Ockenga's Revision. I understand Dr. Ockenga revised this part of his book at a later date, perhaps due to pressures from Bible believing people. Many of these neo-evangelicals and some Fundamentalists believe in theistic evolution. They believe that God made a sub-man or beast. This beast evolved to a certain point, and then God just breathed into that beast the breath of life. This is untrue!

- **2. THE SOUL.**

    (2:7b) : *". . . and breathed into his nostrils the BREATH OF LIFE; and man became a LIVING SOUL."*

    a. The REAL "you," (your spirit and soul) is unseen by others.

- **3. THE SERVICE.**

    (2:15): *"And the Lord God took the MAN, and put him into the garden of Eden TO DRESS IT AND TO KEEP IT."*

> a. It was Adam who had to keep the garden of Eden.

So, today, it is the responsibility of the MAN to work and to SUPPORT his family. It seems that often in today's world, the man has failed the husbandly responsibility.

- **4. THE SELECTIVITY.**

    (2:16-17): *"And the Lord God commanded the MAN, saying, Of every tree of the garden thou mayest freely eat: (2:17)* **but** *of the tree of the knowledge of good and evil, thou shalt not eat of it: for in the day that thou eatest thereof thou shalt surely die."*

> a. God put a boundary on the fruit trees in the garden of Eden (v. 9).

There was a choice. All the fruit was beautiful and delicious. They could eat from all but ONE of those fruit trees. God gave these boundaries. There was beautiful fruit. There was delicious fruit. The Bible does not tell us what kind of fruit it was. The only thing we know is that this fruit was edible. Every type of berry, every type of thing that you can think of that was good could be eaten. God said there was a boundary. Adam and Eve had to make a selection. They had to stay away from the *"tree of the knowledge of good and evil."*

- **5. THE SOLITUDE.**

    (2:18a): *"And the Lord God said, It is NOT GOOD that the MAN SHOULD BE ALONE; . . ."*

> a. God didn't want the man to be alone.

Animals weren't the answer. Some perverted minds and bodies today practice the sin of bestiality. They mate with beasts or animals. Another man was not the answer. God hates the sin of sodomy and homosexuality which is rampant today. That was not God's intent. It's not good for man to be alone. Some men who are single are alone. If this is God's *"gift"* to that man, it is all right (1 Corinthians 7:7). In the beginning, God said it was not good. This is why He created Eve for Adam.

- **6. THE SOLUTION.**

    (2:18b-20): *"I will make him an HELP MEET for him. (2:19) And out of the ground the Lord God formed every beast of the field, and every fowl of the air; and brought them unto Adam to see what he would call them: and whatsoever Adam called every living creature, that was the name thereof. (2:20) And Adam gave names to all cattle, and to the fowl of the air, and to every beast of the field; but for Adam there was NOT found an HELP MEET FOR HIM."*

a. God wanted a help "meet" or SUITABLE.

God wanted a suitable mate or helper for Adam. That was God's solution. God didn't find such a mate in any of the animal kingdom. No bird, no bee, no fish, no cattle, no monkey, no leopard, no lion, no tiger, nor any other animal was a suitable mate for man.

- **7. THE SURGERY.**

    (2:21-22 a): (2:21) *"And the Lord God caused a deep sleep to fall upon Adam, and he slept: and he took one of his ribs, and closed up the flesh instead thereof; (2:22) And the rib, which the Lord God had taken from man, made he a WOMAN . . ."*

    Adam Was Asleep. The first anesthetic was made by the Lord Himself. He put man into a *"deep sleep"* and took that rib out of Adam in order to make Eve. Notice that He made a woman from the rib of the man. He did not make another man. He was not fostering homosexuality or sodomy.

    Not Another Animal. He did not make another animal, fostering the sin of bestiality. He made the woman for the MAN, NOT for ANOTHER WOMAN. Lesbianism is condemned by God (Romans 1:26). This is a blasphemous sin which is on the rise today. It is being glorified by prominent people and on television. God made one woman for the one man. She complemented that man.

- **8. THE SOLEMNIZING.**

    (2:22b): *". . . and brought her unto the man."*

a. God brought Eve unto the man.

This was the first marriage. It was solemnized by God Himself. It took place in the Garden of Eden. God was the One who was the Master of Ceremonies.

Chapter One—The Maker of a Melodious Marriage

● **9. THE STRATEGY.**
(2:23): *"And Adam said, This is now bone of my bones, and flesh of my flesh: she shall be called woman, because she was taken out of Man. (2:24) Therefore shall a man LEAVE his father and his mother, and shall CLEAVE unto his wife; and they shall be ONE FLESH."*

a. The Bible says we are to "LEAVE" our parents.

How to "Leave." If you do not leave your parents physically you have to leave them mentally. So many times marriages are spoiled because the wife goes home to Mama or the husband asks more help of his Dad then he should. I know of a young man who was married for a few years, but his Dad continued to support him and his wife. This is not going to teach this young man anything as far as a home and responsibilities are concerned. He is a spoiled boy. This practice could result in great calamity.

Apron Strings. This is what some fathers do and this is what some sons do, but God said to cut the apron strings and leave. It does not mean you never go back and see Mom and Dad. This does not mean you don't love them, but that means you must leave. Some stay on the farm because it is a family farm. I know the Amish do that and some others, but in heart you have to leave.

b. The Bible says we are to "CLEAVE" to our wife.

Marriage Break-Ups. There is to be permanency in marriage. It must be one man and one woman until death parts them. You must stick to your marriage with tenacity and perseverance. That's what this word *"cleave"* means. You must hold on to your wife, not someone else's wife.

        (1) 1900----1 marriage in 12 ended in divorce (8%).
        (2) 1940----1 marriage in 6 ended in divorce (17%).
        (3) 1970's--1 marriage in 3 ended in divorce (33.3%).
        (4) 1980's--1 marriage in 2 ended in divorce (50%).
        (5) 1990----1 marriage in 2 ended in divorce (50%).
        (6) 1995----1 marriage in 2 ended in divorce (50%).
        (7) 2003----1 marriage in 2 ended in divorce (50%)
        [projected as of date of publication]

Rampant Divorce. Notice that in 2003, 50% of all who stood before a minister and took the vows of marriage have had their marriages end in divorce. Though divorce is much too high among born-again Christians, I would hope that percentage is not true for Christian marriages. I've been told that the divorce rate among Christians is on a par with the unsaved world. In our times, many don't even bother getting married, as you know. They just "shack up." Today there are so many sexually transmitted diseases abounding. The Lord, I think, must be getting restless in Heaven and is starting to clamp down on those who are flaunting marriage and not doing that which is right. The plague and judgment of God is upon us in this day and age in which we live.

> **c. One Flesh.**

That is the sexual aspect of marriage (1 Corinthians 7:1-5) which we'll take up later in the lessons.

C. A Shame (Genesis 3).

● 1. THE SUSCEPTIBILITY.
(Genesis 3:1-6a): (3:1) *"Now the serpent was more subtil than any beast of the field which the Lord God had made. And he said unto the WOMAN, Yea, hath God said, Ye shall not eat of every tree of the garden? . . . (3:6a) . . . she TOOK of the fruit thereof, and DID EAT, . . ."*

> **a. The WOMAN (NOT the man) was seduced (tempted) by the serpent.**

God told the MAN, "*THOU shalt not eat of it.*" (2:16-17). This is a fact. I'm not making this up. It is in the Word. He didn't say "*ye shall not eat*" He said, "*Thou shalt not eat.*" He was talking to Adam. Our King James Bible makes that difference very clear. "Ye" is a nominative case. It is always used as the subject of a verb. It is always plural, meaning more than one person. "Thou," on the other hand, is always singular, meaning only one person. To my knowledge no other version in the English language makes this distinction clearly, so there is no question. You don't have to know Hebrew. You don't have to know Greek. You have to know only English and the grammatical rules used in 1611 in the Bible. I repeat, God did not say "*ye shall not eat.*" He said, "*Thou shalt not eat.*" He talked to Adam. Apparently, Eve was not there when God said this. Satan used this trick as he tempted the woman. Satan told her it was all right to eat of all the fruit in the garden

● 2. THE SIN.
(3:6b) : *". . . and gave also unto her HUSBAND with her; and HE DID EAT."*

Chapter One–The Maker of a Melodious Marriage

> a. The sin of man, *"he did eat."* (Romans 5:12, 14-- Adam's Sin)

(1 Timothy 2:13-14) (2:13) *"For Adam was first formed, then Eve. (2:14) And Adam was NOT DECEIVED, but the woman being deceived was in the transgression."*

> b. Adam DID sin, however.

● **3. THE SHAME.**
(3:7): *"And the eyes of them both were opened, and THEY KNEW THAT THEY WERE NAKED; and they sewed fig leaves together, and made themselves aprons."*

> a. Aprons required sewing.

The fig leaves were a substitute for innocency and uprightness. In Genesis 2:25 Adam and Eve were naked, and they were not ashamed. Some feel God clothed them with a cloud of glory. The shame came because of their sin. The glory departed. It says: *"And they were both NAKED, the MAN and his WIFE, and were not ashamed."*

> b. God asked them a question.

Genesis 3:11: *"And He said, Who told thee that THOU WAST NAKED? . . ."*)

● **4. THE SHIFTING.**
(3:12-13): (3:12) *"And the MAN said, The WOMAN whom thou gavest to be with me, SHE gave me of the tree, and I did eat. (3:13) And the Lord God said unto the WOMAN, What is this that thou hast done? And the woman said, The SERPENT beguiled me, and I did eat."*

> a. Shifting of blame.

They were individually responsible for their actions. (Cf. Deuteronomy 24:16): *"The fathers shall not be put to death for the children, neither shall the children be put to death for the fathers: EVERY MAN SHALL BE PUT TO DEATH FOR HIS OWN SIN."*

> b. I'm sure we have all been guilty of shifting blame in our marriages.

Don't say "The Devil made me do it." This may be true, but it also may be our flesh that makes us do wrong. You and I are responsible for our own sins that we do with our mouth, our hands, our whole bodies, our minds, and our thoughts. Yet, often, our personal sins affect those whom we love. Everyone casts a shadow on family and friends! Both Adam and Eve were guilty of their own sins and responsible to God for their own actions. It may be true that someone may influence you to be bad, but God says you acted this way, therefore you are responsible. You cannot shift the blame in God's eyes.

- **5. THE SENTENCE.**
    (3:14-19) (3:14) *"And the Lord God said unto the SERPENT. . . (3:16) Unto the WOMAN He said . . . (3:17) And unto ADAM He said . . . cursed is the GROUND . . ."*

> a. Judgment.

There was a judgment:
- (1) on the SERPENT
- (2) on EVE
- (3) on ADAM; and
- (4) on the GROUND.

- **6. THE SUCCESSION.**
    (3:20): *"And Adam called his wife's name EVE; because she was the MOTHER OF ALL LIVING."*

> a. Eve was to be the Mother of all Living.

Eve's Descendants. There is a succession of life. Everyone of us is a descendant from Adam and Eve. This was the sentence of judgment that was passed on to Adam, Eve, and the serpent. Though there may have been a mutuality there before the fall, after the fall the husband would rule over the wife. The wife was to be in submission. This is part of her judgment that was given because of Eve's sin. Adam is not guiltless because he listened to Eve and made the decision to sin. Adam had to toil in the field because of his sin. Because Eve sinned and Adam followed her example, we have a fallen nature. God created Adam from the dust of the ground, and I believe we ought to let the Lord take the dust back to dust. We ought not to hasten it on.

Chapter One—The Maker of a Melodious Marriage

> **b. Let me speak out boldly against cremation.**

Cremation is Heathen. The practice of cremation even involves Christians. Cremation is pagan. The Scriptures show it to be pagan. It's not honoring to God. The Lord Jesus Christ was buried and on the third day He rose again. If any of you have this problem of wanting to be cremated, or you think it would be cheaper to do this, I wish you would get some materials from our Bible For Today bookstore on this area of cremation. Mrs. Waite has made an excellent tape against cremation. It is **BFT #1202**, "What Happens During Cremation?" @ **$4.00 + $1.00 S&H**. She has also made eight broadcasts on her "Just For Women" series. She calls it "Cremation--Is It Christian?" It is **JFW #22** @ **$4.00+$1.00 S&H**.

Get Fraser's Book. One small book is excellent. It is by Fraser. The name of it is *Cremation, Is It Christian?* It is **BFT #233** @ **$3.00 + $2.00 S&H**. He goes into all the pagan cremation acts. You perhaps saw on TV what happened to Mrs. Ghandi. You saw the color and the blaze. They burn all the bodies of the Hindus. I trust that you would let the Lord take your body back to dust.

Deacon Cremated His Wife. When I learned that one of the deacons in the church that I used to be a member of cremated his wife the day after she died, I was shocked. Her body was burned to a crisp. On one occasion, my wife had an interview with a local funeral director. It is an excellent interview. She asked questions about what happens during cremation. He gave her all the details and told her it was a good thing to do. Then she asked the "64-million-dollar-question": *"Are you going to be cremated when you die?"* He was selling cremation for other people, but when it came to himself he said "NO!" He said he was going to be buried.

Crematory Interview. We stopped at the burial place of Fanny Crosby because my wife has been giving "The Tribute to Fanny Crosby" since 1978. Fanny Crosby's grave is in Bridgeport, Connecticut. In that cemetery was a crematory. We talked to the caretaker who was in the crematory. He showed us all the ovens where the bodies were burned up. My wife asked him: *"When the time comes for you to die are you going to be cremated?"* He said : *"Oh no, not me, I am going to be buried."*

Toes Hurt? If I've stepped on anybody's toes please pardon me, but it is in the Scriptures. You look and study this out for yourself. Burial is Christian, cremation is heathen.

● 7. THE SACRIFICE.

(3:21) : *"And unto Adam also and to his wife did the Lord God make COATS OF SKINS, and clothed them."*

a. Coats of skins.

Blood had to be shed to get these skins. There are three things that God was teaching us in His clothing Adam and Eve with skins. I remember what Dr. M. R. DeHaan used to say about this first sacrifice in the Bible. He was the founder of the Radio Bible Class. He also taught a Detroit Bible class every Friday. I attended these classes while I was a student at the University of Michigan in Ann Arbor. Dr. DeHaan taught:

Lessons From the "Coats of Skins"
1. Salvation had to be by death.
2. Salvation had to be by the death of an innocent substitute.
3. Salvation had to be by the shedding of blood. This was how God was showing that the sinless Lord Jesus Christ Who shed His blood and died on the Cross of Calvary is the only sacrifice for sinners.

- **8. THE SERVITUDE.**
  (3:17b,19,23b) : (3:17b) " . . *cursed is the GROUND for thy sake; in sorrow shalt thou eat of it all the days of thy life;* . . (3:19) *In the sweat of thy face shalt thou eat bread, till thou return unto the ground;* . . . (3:23) *Therefore the Lord God sent him forth from the garden of Eden, TO TILL THE GROUND from whence he was taken.*"

a. After the fall, Adam had to labor for his food.

It was hard labor and servitude for the man. The thorns and the thistles made it difficult to grow the food needed to sustain life.

Chapter One—The Maker of a Melodious Marriage

SUMMARY

Here is a summary of facts about "melodious marriage" and its Maker.
1. The **source** was God.
2. The **stamp** upon us was His image, and His likeness.
3. The **separateness** was that they were male and female.
4. The **splendor** was that God blessed them.
5. The **supplication** was for them to be fruitful and multiply.
6. The **substance** was that we are made of dust.
7. The **soul** is the real person that is inside the body that nobody can see but the Lord.
8. The **service** was that Adam had to tend the garden.
9. The **selectivity** was that man could eat of the fruit freely except for one tree.
10. The **solitude** was that it was not good for man to be alone.
11. The **solution** was the creating of woman, Eve, for the man.
12. The **surgery** was preformed while Adam was in a deep sleep.
13. The **solemnizing** was that God brought the woman to the man and pronounced them husband and wife.
14. The **strategy** was leaving parents, cleaving to each other, and thus becoming one flesh.
15. The **susceptibility** showed that Eve was the weaker vessel. Satan knew who to talk to.
16. The **sin** was that Eve ate and then Adam ate of the forbidden tree.
17. The **shame** was that they knew they were naked.
18. The **shifting** of blame was when the woman said the serpent made her do it. The man said the woman made him do it.
19. The **sentence** was placed upon the serpent, the woman, and the man.
20. The **succession** was that Eve would be the mother of living.
21. The **sacrifice** was the coats of skins which point toward the cross of Calvary.
22. The **servitude** was that the sinning man would have to serve as a slave to the ground and the sinning woman would have to submit to her husband.

♥♥♥

Chapter Two
The Managers of a Melodious Marriage

The first chapter discussed "THE **MAKER** OF A MELODIOUS MARRIAGE." The present chapter will discuss: **"THE MANAGERS OF A MELODIOUS MARRIAGE"** If anything is melodious it has to be managed, and there are only two managers of a Christian marriage the Christian husband and the Christian wife

A. The Duties of Christian Wives to Christian Husbands

● 1. THE SUBMISSION:

> (Ephesians 5:22, 24). (5:22) *"WIVES, SUBMIT yourselves unto your own husbands, as unto the Lord . . . . (5:24) Therefore as the church is subject unto Christ, so let the wives be to their own husbands in every thing."*

Submission Is Controversial. In our culture, as soon as you begin to talk about "submission," many women (even **Christian women**) bristle. I trust that none of you ladies will bristle as we think about the Scriptural duty of "submission" as unto the Lord by a Christian wife to a Christian husband. The women's liberation movement of our day is the antithesis of the Biblical teaching of "submission" by the Christian wife to the Christian husband--or even by the Christian wife to a non-Christian husband. Their understanding of what the Christian husband should do for his Christian wife is also the antithesis of Biblical teaching. There is war in our culture.

Submission Not Cultural. Some today among the new evangelicals, and, sad to say, even among some of those who consider themselves Fundamentalists, teach that "submission" is only a cultural command which does not apply to us today. These teachers falsely say that, though in Paul's day the women were in submission to men, we don't have to obey this today. They teach that this is a cultural command that need not be obeyed. This form of Biblical interpretation is extremely deadly to God's truth. If this interpretive method is thought to be valid in this instance, why could it not be thought to be valid in a multitude of other New Testament doctrines?

Christian Women Should "*Submit.*" Christian women should be thoroughly grounded on their role in "submission" to their husbands well before they come to their marriage ceremony. I was told about a young woman who was counseled Scripturally about submission to her husband, and she backed out of that marriage. Christian women should learn that they are to submit to their husbands as it says in this verse. Remember, you wives are to submit yourselves unto your own husbands, not to someone else's husband.

Do God's Will. Christian wives, do you submit yourselves unto the Lord Jesus Christ? Do you want His will in your life? Do you wish to please Him? This is the issue right here. If you Christian wives know what it is to submit to the Lord Jesus Christ, you should know how to submit to your own husbands.

"*Obey*" Left Out. Many marriage ceremonies these days omit the word, "*obey*" in the marriage vows. Obedience is left out because of the timidity and the fearfulness of the preachers to preach the Words of God. As I said before, many women get angry when it comes to the subject of their "submission" to their husbands.

False Doctrine on This. I want to point out also that Ephesians 5:21 has led some Christians to a false doctrine in regard to submission and the role of Christian husbands and wives as the managers of a "melodious marriage." Ephesians 5:20-21 reads:

"*Giving thanks always for all things unto God and the Father in the name of our Lord Jesus Christ;* **Submitting yourselves one to another** *in the fear of God.*"

"*Mutual Submission*" **Unscriptural**. Recently, many Bible-believing Christians have used verse 21 to teach what they term "*mutual submission*" between Christian husbands and Christian wives. This verse does not mean that. It means we are to have a submissive spirit in all of our relationships. We are to defer to others, and not always to think of ourselves alone.

Then Paul went on in the next few verses and specified various groups of pairs where one of the pairs should be submissive to the other pair. Verse 21 is merely the topic sentence to teach submission to proper people.

Beware of This Error. Beware of the false teaching of "*mutual submission*." Maybe your preachers teach this. I hope they don't. We must be strong against that. The teaching is false. When taken to its logical conclusion, this teaching believes that the Christian husband must submit to the Christian wife and the Christian wife must submit to her husband. It also would apply to

Ephesians chapter 6. The parents must submit to the children, and the children must submit to the parents; the masters must submit to the servants, and the servants must submit to the masters.

No One in Charge. The problem with this teaching is that if you have everyone submitting to each other, who is going to be in charge? Who is going to make the decisions in the home? As I said before, this false teaching is called *"mutual submission."* When you hear this *"mutual submission"* on Christian radio programs or read about it in Christian books, don't believe it.

Devil's Compromise. This is a compromise of the Devil in these last days in which we live. I believe this is an accommodation to the women's movement which puts women in charge of men. This is inverting God's order which goes all the way back to the Garden of Eden.

Garden of Eden Change. There might have been a *"mutual submission"* in the Garden of Eden before the fall. It is possible. One thing we do know is that Eve fell, left God's will, and took of the forbidden fruit in the garden of Eden. It was the tree of the knowledge of good and evil. She gave it to Adam and he fell also and took of this forbidden fruit. After this event, there was a definite change. In Genesis 3:16, God said unto the woman:

> *". . . Thy desire shall be toward thy husband and **he shall rule over thee**."*

Eve Judged. This indicates that, possibly, it wasn't that way before. God said, since this happened, Eve had to be in subjection to her own husband, Adam. Here is the teaching in verse 21 which we must realize in context. It is "submission" in general and not in the husband and wife relationship.

Paul Is Plain-Spoken. Paul does not mince words. He just goes right out and talks about the home. In verses 22 and 24, he stated:

> *"Wives, submit yourselves unto your own husbands, as unto the Lord. . . .(v. 24) Therefore as the church is subject unto Christ, so let the wives be to their own husbands in every thing."*

He is writing to Christians here at Ephesus. This is a Christian context. Christian wives are to be in subjection to their Christian husbands just like all Christians are to be subject unto Christ.

> **a.** *HupotassO* ("submit").
>
> This word means *"to obey; be under obedience; put under; subject to; in subjection to; submit oneself to."* In Ephesians 5:22 & 24. This word also means *"to command, to order to arrange."* Wives are to arrange themselves under the leadership of their husbands. Wives are under the protective care of their husbands. They are under his rulership. This word is also used in Colossians 3:18: *"Wives, **submit** yourselves unto your own husbands, as it is fit in the Lord."*

Meaning of "Submit." In Greek, the verb, *"submit,"* is in the present tense and the imperative mood. This means that the Christian wives are commanded *"to continually submit themselves"* unto their own husbands.

Other Uses. This word is also used in 1 Peter 3:1-6 (3:1) *"Likewise, ye WIVES, BE **IN SUBJECTION** to your own husbands;.. (3:5) For after this manner in the old time the holy WOMEN also, who trusted in God, adorned themselves, being **IN SUBJECTION** UNTO THEIR OWN HUSBANDS: (3:6) even as SARA OBEYED ABRAHAM, calling him Lord: whose daughters ye are, . . ."*

Winning Husbands. Many wives have won their husbands to the Lord Jesus Christ because of their obedience and submission unto them. Here is that word *hupotassO* ("submit") again.

> **b.** *HupakouO* ("obey").
>
> This word means *"to listen, to harken, used of one who on the knock at the door comes to listen who it is, the duty of a porter; to harken to a command; to obey, be obedient to, submit to"*

Sarah "Obeyed." Some Bible teachers have said that the Bible never tells Christian wives to obey their husbands. They say that it is only commanded that children obey their parents. They are wrong. *"Sarah obeyed Abraham."* Apparently, these teachers have forgotten that Sarah is used as an example to Christian wives of **obedience** to their husbands. She called him *"lord."*

Sarah Wrongly Used. Speaking of Sarah, there is a group of feminists and lesbians who had (and may still have) a paper called *"Daughters of Sarah."* Here are homosexuals who are sinners in the eyes of God who are using Sarah's good name. They are besmirching Sarah's name by calling themselves *"Daughters of Sarah."* These women leaders of this group are not in subjection or obedience to any man. In fact, they are men-haters. These people are called "misanthropes." *"MISO"* is the Greek word for *"hate,"* and *"ANTHROPOS"* is the Greek word for "*man.*" These kind of women are man-haters. Misanthropic people are those who hate men. The lesbians in these so-called gay rights people fit into this category.

A Lesbian Paper. My wife used to get this paper called, "*Daughters of Sarah.*" Virginia Mollenkott, and others, wrote in that paper. Mollenkott holds a Ph.D. in English and teaches in the English Department in Patterson State College in New Jersey. My wife had an interview on tape with lesbian Virginia Mollenkott before she came "out of the closet." My wife went all the way to California to report on a feminist conference held in Pasadena.

An Interview Assignment. One of the assignments that I gave Mrs. Waite was to interview Virginia Mollenkott. My wife is 5'2", and Virginia Mollenkott is much taller and built somewhat like a football player. My wife's interview is an interesting tape (**BFT #697 @ $4 + $1 S&H**). My wife asked her if she were a lesbian. Virginia Mollenkott thought that was a very rude question, but she didn't give her a "yes" or "no" answer. Mrs. Mollenkott said that if she said she was a lesbian, that would alienate her friends who were straight people. If she said she was not a lesbian that would alienate her lesbian friends. By her answer, she conveyed the fact that she was a lesbian. A few years later, she came out boasting that she has been, and is, a lesbian. She is proud of it.

Five Years Active Duty. In my five years on active service in the Navy I had between 3,000 to 4,000 counseling sessions. I'll never forget one homebreaker. A marine came in when I was with the Marine Corps Air Station in Opalocka, Florida. This marine told me that his home was breaking up and that his wife was leaving him. I asked him what the problem was. He told me that she was leaving him for another **woman** rather than the usual problem with another **man**. That was one of my first introductions to a woman breaking up the home of a man.

Repetition of This Sin. I've seen this repeated in a pastor's home in New Jersey in a church affiliated with the General Association of Regular Baptist Churches (GARBC). This pastor, in North Jersey, was separated from his wife many years. The cause of this was his wife left him for another woman. Husbands, guard your wives.

Billy James Hargis. It brings to mind Billy James Hargis's excuse for his homosexual relations. He said he could not help it. He said that his genes and chromosomes were responsible for it. It is like comedian Flip Wilson's statement when he would say, "The devil made me do it." There is no excuse for our sins against our mates and the Lord. We must keep our homes melodious and happy.

"**Subjection.**" The word, "subjection," (*hupotassO*) is also used in 1 Timothy 2:11-12). (2:11) "*Let the WOMAN learn in silence with all SUBJECTION. (2:12) But I suffer not a woman to teach, nor to usurp authority over the man, but to be in silence.*"

Christian Woman's Role. This is all a part of the Christian woman's role in her Christian marriage and in the church. They are to be "*silent*" and in "*subjection.*" That's why I don't think it is Biblical and proper for a woman to teach Bible classes with men present. I know there are some women who teach classes or pray where men are present. Some say that their pastor gave them the authority to teach the class. I don't agree with that. You may, and I'll let you hold that view if you would like. I believe you ought to have men teaching men and women in doctrinal and Bible classes. If women would stop teaching, more men would come forward and fill in the gaps!

My Wife Teaches Women. That is why my wife teaches women. She has an excellent paper entitled "*Mandates for Marriage--68 Hints for Women.*" It is **BFT #623 @ $1.50 + $1.00 S&H**. She says they are not for the men; they are only for the women. She has many suggestions wife to wife. She does not want the men to have them. She would never teach men. She feels that is wrong. Her Aunt always taught an adult class of men and women. I don't believe this is either wise or Scriptural--even when the pastor approves.

Women Preachers. We have a friend, from a Baptist church near us, who was supposed to be giving only "a testimony" in a Sunday evening service. She ended up preaching. There is a fine line between a testimony and preaching. We have many women preachers in all these different denominations, including the Baptist denominations. It used to be just the Episcopalians, the Presbyterians, and the Methodists that had women preachers. Now, even some Baptists, especially Southern Baptists, have joined ranks with them. We must hold our ground in opposition to women preachers.

Pastors Must Be Males. The Bible clearly teaches that the pastor-bishop-elder must be "the husband of one wife" (1 Timothy 3:2; Titus 1:6). That clearly rules out women preachers. This doesn't stop these women preachers, does it? They say this was just a cultural command during Paul's time, but it does not apply today. For this reason, they believe that women can preach. This reasoning is defective.

---

c.   "*hupotagei*" from "*hupotassO*" "subjection."

(1 Corinthians 14:34-35) (14:34) "*Let your WOMEN KEEP SILENCE in the churches: for it is not permitted unto them to speak; but they are commanded*

to be UNDER OBEDIENCE, as also saith the law. (14:35) *And if they will learn any thing, let them ask their husbands at home: for it is a shame for women to speak in the church."*

> d. *hupotassesthai* "under obedience." This is the same as in Ephesians 5:22.

Wives' Subjection. This speaks of the subjection that the Christian wife is to have under the Christian husband. There is a difference of opinion on this. Some feel that women can talk in Sunday School class or have questions. Others feel that they should be silent at all times while in the church building. The point that I am making here is this. The restriction of keeping women from taking the ascendancy in the local churches is part of the Christian women's place in subjection to her own husband and in the local church. This is also why we should not have women preachers. This *"being silent"* in the church would certainly disqualify women from being preachers. Sometimes you have women Sunday School teachers who are teaching both women and men. This is not proper. Women should not teach men, but only other women and children.

- **2. THE SUBORDINATION:**
    (Ephesians 5:23) *"For the husband is the HEAD OF THE WIFE, even as Christ is the HEAD OF THE CHURCH; and he is the Saviour of the body."*

> The headship of the husband.

"*Head*" Means "Head." The Christian wife is in a subordinating position to her Christian husband as the *"head of the wife."* Lesbian Virginia Mollenkott, in her book, *Women, Men, and the Bible*, states that she does not believe "head" means head. Well, if "head" does not mean head then "body" does not mean body. This is the same word for "head" that is used in the Greek text everywhere in the New Testament. Headship involves a subordination. If you cut the head off a chicken, we are told that the chicken walks around for a little bit in spite of the fact that he has no head. You've heard the expression that you are acting "like a chicken with its head cut off."

Head Controls Our Bodies. If you have a hard blow to the head, your body falls. If you have a hard blow to the head, your eyes can't see right. If you have a hard blow to the head, it could result in your being paralyzed. Your hands or your legs might not be able to function properly. Many things could happen when your head is injured. The brain tells every other part of your body what to do. It controls the autonomic nervous system, and the central nervous system. This is what headship means. It involves control. People sometimes facetiously say that the husband is the head, but the wife is like the neck. She can influence the head. That's all right.

- **3. THE SEVERITY:**

   (5:33b) *"... and the WIFE see that she REVERENCE her husband."*

---
phobEtai for "reverence."

This word means *"to frighten; to be alarmed; to be in awe of; i.e. revere; be (sore) afraid; fear (exceedingly); reverence."*

The Meaning of "*Reverence*." There is fear involved with this word, "*reverence.*" Not that a wife is to cower to her husband, but there is an element of "*fear*" in here. That word, *phobEtai*, means "*fear*" as well as "*awe.*" Just like the "*fear of the Lord*" really means "*fear.*" Some people soften that. The Old Testament uses the expression "*fear God*" (Job 1:9; Psalm 66:16) or the "*fear of the Lord*" (Psalm 111:10). Some say that this means only to have a "reverential trust." That may be a part of it, but in that Hebrew expression as well as in this Greek expression, it involves real, genuine "*fear.*" I "*fear*" God. God is powerful. He is much more powerful than I. That's why He wants us to stay in line.

The Meaning of "*Fear*." I love the Lord, but I also "*fear*" God. Wives should have a healthy respect and a "*fear*" of their own husbands. Not in a bad sense, but in a sense that it is used here in Scripture in the word, "*reverence.*" I must point it out because it is in Scripture. You may differ with me on this.

B. The Duties of Christian Husbands to Christian Wives.

Now For Husbands. Paul takes up next the husbands and their duties. They, along with the wives, are also an important member of the team of managers for a "melodious marriage." You husbands might ask how often you should tell your wife to be in "submission" to you. You don't have to mention that. I have never had to mention that to my wife in months. [laughter] On occasion, but very seldom, do I have to remind her of this. My wife has a lot of ingenuity. She is a go-getter. She is an independent thinker. She has to be held down a little bit. Sometimes she is like a wild horse that has to be reined in. It is a question of attitude. You don't have to keep reminding people of these things. Some wives, though you remind them a hundred times, it does not do them a bit of good. They don't have a submissive spirit. It's a spiritual thing that they have to settle before the Lord. There are some women who are naturally built to be dynamic leaders. It is hard for them to understand and to follow this Scriptural injunction.

- **1. THE SUPERINTENDENCY:**
  (Ephesians 5:23) *"For the husband is the HEAD of the wife, even as Christ is the HEAD of the church: and he is the saviour of the body."*

> **The headship for the husband.**

Home Headship. The Christian husband is the head, or the superintendent, in a "melodious marriage." Woe unto us who are Christian husbands if we don't have our head screwed on right, or if we don't have it all-together, or if we don't have the ability to lead and make decisions. There are some men that way, and their wives have to give them some assistance. Even so, Christian wives still have to be in subjection to their husbands even when they give them assistance. Sometimes the husbands call for such assistance. When the assistance is given, I trust it will be given in a sweet, "submissive" manner.

- **2. THE SACRIFICE:**
  (5:25, 33a) *"Husbands, love your wives, even as Christ also **LOVED** the church and **GAVE** HIMSELF for it; . . . Nevertheless let every one of you in particular so LOVE his wife even as himself; . . ."*

> ***"Love"*** **and** ***"gave"*** **are two important words.**

Love Involves Sacrifice. When you talk about Christian husbands loving their wives and giving themselves as Christ gave Himself for us, you are talking about sacrifice. A Christian husband has to provide everything for his Christian wife and has to sacrifice for her. If need be, he has to scrimp and save and deprive himself of something he would like to have. He has to give himself to that wife because God's Word says he has to do this. He has to do this just as the wife has to do what the Lord requires of her. Remember, as we said before, marriage is a duet and not a solo. It is not two soloists singing a different song. It's a duet, an arrangement that must be worked out in harmony, if it is to be a "melodious marriage." The husband must sacrificially give of himself to his wife.

- **3. THE SANCTIFICATION:**
    (5:26-27) *"That he might SANCTIFY and CLEANSE it with the WASHING of water by the Word, (5:27) That he might present it to himself a GLORIOUS church, NOT having SPOT, or WRINKLE, or ANY SUCH thing; but that it should be HOLY and WITHOUT BLEMISH."*

> **Cleansed, washed, glorious, no spot, no wrinkle, holy, without blemish.**
> This is speaking of the Lord Jesus, but we as Christian husbands have the same injunction, *"for the husband is the HEAD of the wife, even as Christ is the HEAD of the church: . . ."*

Cleansing Needed. Just as the Lord Jesus Christ wants to cleanse His redeemed people, so the husband should desire that his Christian wife be cleansed, be glorious, be without spot, be without wrinkle, and be holy. It is a sad disgrace when a Christian wife defiles herself with some sin that is notorious and questionable. I think of a pastor in another state who called me recently whose wife has been seeing a young boy. She is in her 40's and the young boy is in his 20's. Maybe there is not fornication and adultery [yet], but it just doesn't look right. This pastor's church sees this and wonders what she is doing with this boy. This is besmirching the character of the pastor's wife. She is to be holy. She is not to be spotted or wrinkled. You remember all the scandals of the PTL leaders. This is terrible.

Husbands Should Be Concerned. We husbands have a sanctification in our marriage that should concern us. We need to try to keep our wives clean and holy. We must do our part to encourage this cleanliness so that our wives can be without blemish. Sometimes it takes more of a husband's time than he would like to give, but think of the reward as well as saving that marriage in the long-run.

- **4. THE SELFISHNESS:**
    (5:28-30) (5:28) *"So ought men to love their wives AS THEIR OWN BODIES. He that loveth his wife loveth HIMSELF. (5:29) For no man ever yet hated his own flesh; but nourisheth and cherisheth it, even as the Lord the church: (5:30) For we are members of his body, of his flesh, and of his bones."*

I call it *"selfishness"* because if you love your own body that is selfish, yet this is what God tells us is the case. In this area of selfishness there are two divisions. There is a schooling and there is a sheltering.

> **a. Schooling.**
> The Greek word for *"nourisheth"* is *ektrephei*. It means *"to rear up to maturity; to cherish or train; to bring up or nourish"* We love ourselves, husbands, so we ought to love our wives like we love our own selves.

Husbands don't purposely hurt themselves by falling down and breaking their legs. They don't cut themselves with a knife. The same should be true for husbands' love for their wives. God tells us that a man's wife is a member of his body. She is one flesh with him. That word, *"nourish,"* has to do with schooling. A man is to *"nourish"* his wife like she were in a school. He should attempt to bring her to maturity in the things of the Lord. When a man starts caring for and protecting another woman, in the manner God tells him to do for his own wife, he should recognize it as sin and stop it before he is trapped.

> **b. Sheltering.**
> The Greek word for *"cherisheth"* is *thelpei* from the verb *thalp0*. It means *"to warm; to brood; to foster; to cherish."*

This is like a chicken who is brooding and warming her young chicks. The sheltering part of a Christian husband to his Christian wife involves his provision of warmth and shelter for her. As a Christian husband, we are to school, to help, and to train as well as to shelter our wife. This is part of the selfishness in treating them just as we would our own bodies.

- **5. THE SEPARATION.**
    (5:31a) *"For this cause shall a man LEAVE his father and mother, . . ."*

This is a principle that was taught in Genesis 2:24. This separation involves leaving your father and your mother. It involves making a break with your parents in the sense of not being dependant on them any longer. In Christian marriage, you need to be your own separate unit. There was an old custom when the parents had a farm that they gave their children a part of that land. Often the older couple moves out of the big farm house and moves into a small addition to the house made for them. The Amish still have this practice. The children do not leave spatially, but even in that situation, there should be a leaving in the heart and in the mind. There needs to be a severing. You are an independent unit. Husbands and wives need to be independent of their parents even though they still love them; always they are to leave them.

- **6. THE STICKING:**
    (5:31b) *". . . and shall be JOINED unto his wife . . ."* I stay "sticking" because of what cleaving means.

Cleaving is like GLUE.

No Double Standard. The Christian husband is not to be footloose and fancy-free. He must not have two standards. He should not commit adultery nor should his wife commit adultery. The standard is the same for both husband and wife. We are to glue and stick ourselves to our wives. This is like a bonding cement that cannot be severed. Only death should sever that bond. That's what the sticking and gluing means.

Thoughts of Leaving. What if I were to ask Christian men and Christian women who have been married any length of time, if there was anytime that they have thought in their minds that they would like to leave their mates? What would the answers be? If they are honest I think they would say "yes" to that question. This does not mean that they would leave their mate, but did they ever think about it? Some of you, perhaps, have had an easy road and it has never crossed your mind to leave your mate. Others have had a time when your mate has gotten so much on your nerves that you have wished that you could leave. Maybe you might not have thought of leaving in the sense of divorce, but perhaps just wanting to get away from them for a short time.

"Agape" Love Needed. We must have a love that is an "agape" type of love. This is a Divine love. We must be joined unto our wives. We must stick to our wives. This is a pledge that should be settled before you even enter marriage. I believe there are at least three mandates required for husbands and wives to stick to their marriages.

Three Marriage Mandates

(1) **Both the man and the woman** must be saved. It is unscriptural for a preacher to marry people who are not born-again Christians.

(2) **Both the man and the woman** should be fully dedicated to the Lord Jesus Christ, lock, stock and barrel. To have the best possibility of "sticking" to the marriage, the man and the woman must be 100% yielded and dedicated to the Saviour.

(3) **Both the man and the woman** should have a firm commitment without any question that they are going to stick together like glue until death parts them. They should not even have one thought of divorce. Nothing should enter to break that tie. You say well that takes maturity doesn't it? Well, maybe it does take maturity, but it also takes dedication, will, and a vow.

Chapter Two—The Managers of a Melodious Marriage

Christian Divorces. I am sorry to say that altogether too many people do not worry about their wedding vows these days. They just take them and then break them. In the United States of America in 1995, and even in the projection for 2003, one marriage out of every two ended in divorce. Christians are part of that statistic. They are not a large part, but their numbers are growing. We must get Christian couples to have a deeper commitment to the Lord and to their marriage.

Marriage Like a Ship. I like to look at Christian marriage as being in a ship out in the vast ocean. When I was a Naval Chaplain for five years on active duty, one of my duties involved being in the military sea transportation service (MSTS). That was after I returned from Okinawa where I served the Lord for twelve months without my wife and children. I served for one year with the military sea transportation service. We took army troops from Brooklyn, NY to Bremerhaven, Germany and Southhampton, England. I liken sticking to Christian marriage to the sticking to the huge military sea transportation ship out in the ocean when the storms come. The ship has life boats, yes. It would be folly to go out in a small life boat (unless the ship were sinking fast). It would be much safer to stay in the ship during such storms.

Atlantic Storms. I remember several storms on the Atlantic Ocean. During this time of storm, we had the largest attendances in our Bible classes and preaching services. People had a fear of dying. I remember one Jewish woman who professed faith in Christ. I don't know if she was really saved. She asked me if I thought the ship were going to sink. I told her that I didn't think so. The captain told me that the ship was able to list (tilt) to 38 degrees. I think it was only listing to about 25 degrees, so we have a few more degrees before we go roll over. This storm was good for Chaplain's Bible studies. Marriage should not be like going out in the Atlantic Ocean in a little life boat by yourself. You should stick to the big ship that is going to carry you through. Forsaking the ship, no matter how rough the sea, is dangerous and very likely deadly in the middle of that huge ocean.

Sink or Float. Marriage is like a ship. You either sink or float. You must either sink together or you must float together. You have joys and trials, but you are together and you must stick to it. Christian husbands, if your wife might get a little bit shaky, **it is your job to strengthen the marriage glue** and to see that the cement holds together. Whatever it takes, we who are Christian husbands must be big enough, loving enough, and able enough to achieve this. Sometimes the ladies might seem to have their glue not sticking very much any more, you Christian husbands must make sure that your glue keeps holding. You must continue to "cleave" to your wife.

- **7. THE SEXUALITY:**
    (5:31c) *". . . and they two shall be ONE FLESH."*

> **"One flesh."**

We'll take this up in detail in a later chapter. The *"one flesh"* must be a part of our Christian marriages.

- **8. THE SENSIBILITY:**
    (1 Peter 3:7) *"Likewise, ye husbands, dwell with them according to KNOWLEDGE, giving honour unto the wife, as unto the weaker vessel, and as being heirs together of the grace of life; that your PRAYERS be not hindered."*

> **Christian husbands must be SENSIBLE.**
> They must dwell with their Christian wives with KNOWLEDGE. They must give honor to their wives as being the "weaker vessels."

Husbands' Sensitivity. Husbands must be both sensible and sensitive. They must dwell *"according to knowledge"* with their wives. You Christian husbands know what the weaknesses of your wives are. You know what their frailties are. You must be sensitive to these things *"that your prayers be not hindered."* It is important that this be the case. The knowledge that we have of weaknesses will stave off many difficulties that will come along throughout your Christian marriage.

Women's Liberation. Secular women's liberation women don't think that they are in any sense the *"weaker vessel."* Even the so-called Christian women's liberation women object to that term. I frankly don't believe there is such a thing as a "Christian" Women's Liberation Movement. They call it that, but I don't believe it is "Christian." I talked to one of these women. I said *"I'm sorry, but it's right here in 1 Peter 3:7 where it says that the woman is the weaker vessel."* The woman said, *"We women are not weak. We are just as strong as men."*

The *"Weaker Vessel."* In what sense is the woman the *"weaker vessel"*? In answer to this, I always point to athletic contests. If you consult the *World Almanac*, you can see both the records and the record-holders for such events as the high jump, the pole vault, the 440-yard dash, the 220-yard dash, the 100-yard dash, and so on. I looked at the records for the men including their times and their distances. I also looked at the parallel records for the women.

Chapter Two—The Managers of a Melodious Marriage

Always, in every instance, and without a single exception, the record-holders in the world are the men rather than the women. That doesn't mean that some women aren't stronger then some men. For example, some women can lift more weights than some men. The overall picture, however, is that the women truly are the "weaker vessel" as measured by athletic world-records. The overall picture is that women are the *"weaker vessel"* as the Scripture teaches.

Not Mental Weakness. This doesn't mean that the Christian women are *"weaker"* in their minds. It doesn't mean they are weaker in initiative. It doesn't mean they are weaker in spiritual things. It doesn't mean they are weaker in bearing pain. They bear children. I am very glad to let my wife be the mother of our five children.

First Labor Room. The first child we had, D. A., Junior, was born in 1949. He has two daughters. I remember, when we lived in Dallas, Texas, while I was going to Dallas Theological Seminary, Mrs. Waite gave birth to our first son. That hospital (at least in 1949) permitted husbands to go into the labor room. I'll tell you that was quite an experience. Now, in some instances, husbands are permitted to go into the delivery room. My wife had a difficult delivery with our first son. She had medication that caused her not to remember too much about the delivery and labor. They didn't give me any medication, so I remember it all. The Lord is able to give the women the strength when they need it to bear their children. They are the *"weaker vessel"* so we, as husbands, must remember that and give them honor.

"*More Abundant Honour.*" It says in 1 Corinthians 12:22-24 that *"we give more abundant honour"* to the more *"feeble"* members of our body. Although she is in subjection to her husband, my wife is on my right side when we walk. I was a military man, and military men know that the senior officer always walks on the right and the junior officer walks on the left. I'm her head but I give honor to her. I always open the door for my wife if I can get to it fast enough. It is awkward sometimes, depending on how the door swings. If she is to go ahead of you because she is to be honored and yet you must get ahead of her to open the door without hitting her in the head, it is difficult. We who are Christian husbands do these things because we give honor to our wives whom the Scriptures call *"the weaker vessel"* (1 Peter 3:7). A husband should give his wife emotional support as well as financial support.

Happy Subjection. There is no more happiness in a Christian home in which the wife is in subjection to her husband and the husband loves his wife and gives himself for her as the *"weaker vessel."* There is a great blessing, melody, and harmony in such a home.

● **9. THE SAMPLE:**
(1 Timothy 3:2a, 4a, 5) (3:2a) *"A BISHOP then must be . . . (4 a) One that ruleth well his own house, . . . (3:5) (For if a man*

know not how to rule his own house, how shall he take care of the church of God?)" [For a Pastor-Bishop-Elder]

Pastor's Godly Home. A Bishop (which is another name for a Pastor) must have a godly and orderly home. He must have his wife and his children in the proper order. What about a bishop or pastor who does not *"rule well his own house"*? He would not be a good sample or example of what a Christian home should be. It is important that he *"rules well his own house."* Wives, it is of the utmost importance, if your husband is a pastor, that your house be in order. The same standard is true for *"deacons."*

> **(3:12a)** *"Let the DEACONS be . . . ruling their own houses well."* [For Deacons].

Good Home Standards. Every Christian wife must have a good standard in the home. She must be in subjection to her own husband. She must have a harmonious home if she wants her husband to remain as a pastor or a deacon. The question is what if the man's home is out of line? Should he continue being a pastor? No, he should not, in my judgment. The Scriptures disqualify that man who is out of line in his home.

Pastoral Adultery. Mrs. Waite and I left a former church about two years before its pastor committed adultery with one of the members of the church. He had this adulterous affair over a period of two years. Though he tried to cover it up, it came out into the open. Not only did his family suffer, but the church suffered also.

Neo-Evangelical Pastor. We left previously because he was a neo-evangelical pastor. He went to Dallas Theological Seminary the same as I did, but there was a difference. The seminary was even stronger into neo-evangelicalism when he attended than when I was there. But he drank in that compromise without forsaking it as I did. I was neo-evangelical for some time myself. But when I got out of my five years of active duty as a Naval Chaplain, became the pastor of my first church, and started preaching the Word of God, I found out that I was a Fundamentalist, not a neo-evangelical. When Harold John Ockenga, then the pastor of Boston's Park Street Church, and the other neo-evangelicals in the Boston area began teaching their beliefs, I realized I was a Fundamentalist.

Soft and Unscriptural. The aforementioned pastor of our home church was so soft and unscriptural on so many things that my wife and I couldn't take it anymore. We moved our membership to another Baptist Church closer to our home. As I said before, this pastor carried on an adulterous affair with a married woman in his congregation over a period of two years. When this adultery was uncovered, this pastor thought it was all right for him to continue being the pastor of the church.

Smiling Pastoral Adulterer. I was talking with a lady who was a member of this church at the time when this adultery was discovered. She remembered well when this pastor, after committing adultery for two years, walked into the church business meeting where they were going to decide if he was going to go or stay. He was smiling and shaking hands as if nothing out of line had happened. He almost got to stay in that church. We were told that there were only five votes that made the difference whether he was to leave the church or continue being the pastor. If it weren't for those five people voting against him, he would still be the pastor of that church.

Low Church Morality. Can you imagine the low morality, even the immorality of many in that local church? This church probably had about 600 members in it. This church had such little teaching of the Word of God that it just about let an adulterous pastor continue shepherding that flock. This is the state of affairs that we are in today. That pastor was on the Council of Eighteen in the General Association of Regular Baptist Churches (GARBC) when it happened and during the adultery. You talk about hypocrisy of the highest order, this was it.

Second GARBC Adulterous Leader. A second Council of Eighteen leader of the General Association of Regular Baptist Churches (GARBC) also committed adultery. He thought that he should be a pastor again after this adultery. So he did go back, only to commit a second adultery during this second pastorate. Where do these adulterous men get this idea that they can go back to being a pastor? This is not being an example. It says that the bishop must rule his own house well. He must stay "glued" to his own wife and not go after some other woman.

Two Adulterous Leaders. Here were two leaders (that I know about--there might be others) of the General Association of Regular Baptist Churches were committing adultery while serving on the Council of Eighteen. It makes you wonder, does it not? It shows how subtle such sin is. It grows on the person. They think they are strong. It is like the frog in the hot water who can no longer jump out.

Back Into the Pastorate. This second GARBC adulterous leader sold cars for awhile in another state. Then he was an associate of another pastor. Finally, he became a pastor once again. He became one of the GARBC leaders in that new state. In fact, he was the chairman of the state regional of the GARBC and on that state's Council. After all this, he committed adultery again with one of the women in his church. How many more churches is this man going to go into? There is a standard for the pastor as well as for any member of the church. The man of God, as well as all Christian men, must be a leader in virtuous living.

Another Pastoral Adulterer. I noticed that one prominent man has returned to a Christian ministry since getting out of jail. He was both an adulterer and also reportedly involved in homosexual activities. He was shameful in many ways. Another prominent Christian leader had an assistant who committed adultery with his own sister-in-law. He was fired from that man's school for a period of time, at first. Soon after this, he was brought right back to the school. I don't agree with this. The bishop must be *"blameless"* (1 Timothy 3:2)

Standards Torn to Shreds. The Bible has standards which have been torn to shreds by the world. Some people would say that anything goes. They say that you can do anything you want, be forgiven, and go right on being a leader. No, that is not the way it is. Paul said. *"But I keep under my body, and bring it into subjection: lest that by any means, when I have preached to others, I myself should be a castaway."* Pastors, deacons and other Christian leaders, our home must be very important to us. It is very important to the Lord.

Chapter Three
The Mutuality of a Melodious Marriage

The last two chapters discussed **"THE MAKER OF A MELODIOUS MARRIAGE,"** and "THE **MANAGERS** OF A MELODIOUS MARRIAGE." Now, we want to look at **"THE MUTUALITY OF A MELODIOUS MARRIAGE."** It is not enough to look at the CHRISTIAN WIFE and the CHRISTIAN HUSBAND in isolation. There are many things about which there must be a MUTUALITY.

Before I begin, I would like to read to you an Arabian Proverb. It is an old Proverb that some of you might have heard before. My mother, Helen Waite, quoted it at her 40th class reunion speech (from 1918-1958). I was at Mom's house one summer and saw the poem. I liked it so much that I made copies of it. This proverb is very important in many ways. There are four stanzas.

An Arabian Proverb

"He who knows not, and knows not that he knows not, is a fool.
    Avoid him.
He who knows not, and knows that he knows not, is simple.
    Teach him.
He who knows, and knows not that he knows, is asleep.
    Wake him.
He who knows, and knows that he knows, is a wise man.
    Follow him."

I trust that we all may have the wisdom of Christ on this subject of "**The MUTUALITY** of a Melodious Marriage." I hope that the Scriptures will be your "wise man" tonight in all of these areas of mutuality. My wife, in her *"Mandates For Marriage--68 Hints for Women"* (**BFT #623 @ $1.50**), says, in point number three, that there are three mountains on which marriage is secured. The mountain of Scripture; the mountain of submission; and the mountain of sex.

Three Marriage Mountains
Marriage Mountain #1: Scripture
Marriage Mountain #2: Submission
Marriage Mountain #3: Sex

Geometry. In geometry, we learned that *"three points determine a plane."* So, in Christian marriage, these three points determine the important and vital stability of a Christian marriage.

First Things First. I'm going to take up the mountain of sex first. In a sense, I am going to give you a sex education lesson. We say that sex education should not be taught in the schools because it is taught both immorally and amorally. It is taught wrong and unscripturally. Sex education to our children should be taught primarily in our Christian homes. It should be backed up in our churches. Though the local churches do what they can, they do not generally talk as plainly as I am going to talk about this. God's Word teaches about this subject so I believe we should make it plain to Christian husbands and wives.

Christian Married Couples. We are talking to Christian married couples. Let's see what God has to say about sex education. The question may come to your mind who is it who needs sex education the Scriptural way? Well, those of you who are married one year need it. Those of you who have been married less than one year need it. Those of you who have been married all the way up to 50 years and more need to know what God says about sex education in the marriage as He gives it to us in His Word.

Knowing is one thing. Doing is another.

Do What You Know. It's not enough that you and I know what God says about this subject, we must be obedient and practice what He says. This is a

Chapter Three—The Mutuality of a Melodious Marriage

subject where there must be mutuality in our marriages. Christian wives must do what God teaches here. Christian husbands must do what God teaches here. This subject is taught plainly in God's Word and it should be expounded verse by verse and word by word the same as every other truth of God's Word. I was studying this afternoon with my Greek Testament and Lexicon and I discovered some interesting things.

- **1. THE SEXUALITY.**

    (1 Corinthians 7:1-5) (7:1) *"Now concerning the things whereof ye wrote unto me: It is good for a man not to touch a woman."*

> **a. Meaning of "*Touch*."**
> That Greek word for "*to touch*" has to do with sexual relations.

It is all right if a man doesn't want to "*touch*" or have sexual relations with a woman. In other words, there is no requirement that a man or a woman get married. If they don't want to get married that is all right. That is a possible life choice for them. In Verse 2, Paul warns the Christians at Corinth.

(7:2) *"Nevertheless, to avoid fornication, let every man have his own wife, and let every woman have her own husband."*

> **b. Meaning of "*Fornication*."**
> This Greek word for "*fornication*" is in the plural. It could be literally translated "*to avoid fornications*."

The reason is easy to understand when you think about it for a while. If the sexual needs of either the man or the woman are not met in a Christian marriage there is the possibility of two fornication situations developing, one for the man and one for the woman. It also might be referring to the multiple fornications that would be committed by either the man or the woman because they were not married. The Lord tells us that, to "*avoid fornication*" of any kind, "*Let every man have his own wife, and let every woman have her own husband.*"

> Paul wrote about marriage in **Hebrews 13:4:**
> **"*Marriage is honourable in all, and the bed undefiled: but whoremongers and adulterers God will judge.*"**

> **c. God Is For Marriage.**
> God did not intend for human beings to be like the priests, the monks, and the nuns that pretend not to be married.

As present-day revelations have become public, more frequently than the Roman Catholic Church wants to admit, these priests often have sexual relations with one another, either priests with priests, or priests with girls or women, or priests with young men or small boys in homosexual sin. Also, though less publicized, there are priests who have had sexual relations with the nuns, thus committing heterosexual sin. There are many and various scandals involved there.

> **d. God is Against Homosexuality.**
> This is blasphemy as far as the truth of God is concerned. *"Marriage is honorable in all."*

This does not mean that the nuns should be lesbians and the priests should be homosexuals. Some reports have said that upwards of 40% of the Roman Catholic priests in this country are homosexuals. That is a serious, filthy, rotten mess that we're in isn't it? The Roman Catholic Church is polluted to the hilt. It is not only polluted in doctrine, but also in morals.

> Look at **Hebrews 13:4** again:
> *"Marriage is honourable in all, and the bed undefiled: but whoremongers and adulterers God will judge."*

> **d. The Meaning of "*Bed.*"**
> That Greek word for "*bed*" is "COITE." It is the same root from which we get the English word, "*coitus.*"

It is a reference to the fact that the intimate married, sexual love-relationship is "*undefiled.*" The undefilement in this relationship is limited to the state of "*marriage*" and nothing else. Those who are sexually unfaithful before marriage ("*whoremongers*"), or after marriage ("*adulterers*"), God will judge.

The Groundwork For Marriage. This verse lays the groundwork for Christian marriage and married love. Many Christians (and of course the Roman Catholic Church is chief in this false teaching) believe that the fall of Adam and Eve in the Garden of Eden was when they committed the sexual act.

They believe that this was the forbidden fruit. This is what the Roman Catholic Church teaches. Nothing could be farther from the truth!

Eve Was Beautiful. God made the beautiful woman, Eve, from Adam's rib. Eve was created to be a helper, meet or suitable for Adam's every need. God brought Eve to Adam and said *"Be fruitful, and multiply, and replenish the earth"* (Genesis 1:28). God was the originator of the first marriage and the first marital union.

Married Love Is From God. Some Christians believe (even some Fundamentalists) that we ought to de-emphasize married love. They say, we're holy people. We ought to live in the Spirit, not in the flesh. They say that sexual relations between Christian husbands and Christian wives is carnal and wrong. This teaching is totally wrong and unscriptural. It is not a Biblical position at all.

Beware of False Ideas. I trust none who are reading this booklet believe this false position, either in whole or in part. Nothing could be further from the truth. Just because a person is saved, born-again and has the Holy Spirit of God living in their bodies, is no reason whatever for them to fail to follow the injunction given clearly in 1 Corinthians 7:1-5. We can't say that we are holier than anyone else, and we can get by with violating these verses. Because we are in the flesh, God has made provision for us in the flesh as Christian husbands and wives and we must follow His plan. When husband and wife do not *"come together"* often, they are committing *"sin."* **Continued abstinence and rejection is "sin" in God's sight**. Married couples are to *"come together"* sexually. This is God's plan.

> **e. Avoiding "Fornication."**
> **Paul says in Verse 2 to *"avoid fornication"* both on the part of the man and also on the part of the woman.**

"Let every man have his own wife, and let every woman have her own husband." All you need is one to a customer as they say. You just need one wife or one husband. That is all God's plan has for us and we are to stay married until death. This is an important way God has for avoiding fornication. He doesn't want you to have homosexuality. That's not the way to go. God's plan is that marriage will deliver both men and women from any temptation to fornication. Many Christians at Corinth were guilty of this in the past.

1 Corinthians 6:9 and 11:
> "*Know ye not that the unrighteous shall not inherit the kingdom of God? Be not deceived: neither **fornicators**, nor idolaters, nor **adulterers**, nor **effeminate**, nor abusers of themselves with mankind,* . . . **And such were some of you**: *but ye are washed, but ye are sanctified, but ye are justified in the name of the Lord Jesus, and by the Spirit of our God.*"

Avoiding Bad Things. God wants Christians to avoid all these things. One of the ways to "*avoid fornication*" is to have a faithful Christian marriage. This will be avoided, however, **only** if 1 Corinthians 7:3, 4, and 5 are followed **carefully**. These verses will be explained in detail later in this chapter. It doesn't do a bit a good to have a marriage ceremony and then not follow the rules that God has laid down as far as married love is concerned in these verses.

I would point out that when it says in 1 Corinthians 7:2, "*let every man have his own wife*," that Greek verb that is used is "ECHETO." It is an imperative command in the present tense. It is from the verb, "ECHO." That word means not only "to have" only for a short time, but it means this action of "having and holding" is to be continuous and unending--until death parts the Christian husband and wife.

---

f. To Have and To Hold.
In the marriage ceremony many of us who are pastors use the words, "*Do you take this woman to have and to hold in sickness and in health as long as you both shall live.*"

The word, ECHO, means "*to have and to hold, to embrace, to cling to.*" When the present tense is used in the Greek language, it means that the action is continuous. As we examine 1 Corinthians 7:2-5, we will see about six Greek present tenses that Paul uses. I believe that every one of them has significance.

God's Greek Words Are Inerrant. God makes no mistakes in the Scriptures. The Hebrew and Greek Words were inerrant as they were given and the copies underlying the King James Bible are still inerrant Words. They were "*given by inspiration*" in the originals. The Words were "*God-breathed*" by the Lord Jesus Christ as He gave God the Holy Spirit the exact Words to give to the human writers. In the Greek language you can say that an action occurred just once, or you can say the action is continuous. God chooses in this area of married love to make it a present tense, continuous action. What God means by

Chapter Three—The Mutuality of a Melodious Marriage 43

this is that every Christian husband must *"continue to have, continue to hold, continue to embrace, and continue to cling to his wife."* In the same way, God means that every Christian wife must *"continue to have, continue to hold, continue to embrace, and continue to cling to"* her own husband. This is a continuous action. It is not to stop. So, you never stop your love relations with your husband or with your wife. If you are obedient to Verse 2 then you are continuously having, holding, embracing, and clinging to one another in Christ.

> **(7:3)** *"Let the husband render unto the wife due benevolence: and likewise also the wife unto the husband."*
> The Greek word for *"render"* is the verb, **"APODIDATO."** It is another present tense. It is an imperative command from the verb, **"APODIDOMAI."** It is to be a continuous action. It means *"to give in answer to a claim or expectation."*

> g. Rendering "Due Benevolence."
> Paul is talking about married love in this context. The husband is to *"give"* to his wife *"in answer to a claim"* that she has upon his body in the marriage act, the marriage relation.

This is an *"expectation"* that the wife has. Being in the present tense, it's a continuous *"claim, or expectation."*

"Giving." The same continuous *"giving"* in answer to a *"claim or expectation"* is true for the wife. The wife is to continuously *"give in answer to a claim or expectation"* that her husband has upon her. Notice that this verse addresses the husband first, then the wife.

What is "*Due*"? Then notice what the Christian husband is to render unto the wife. It is *"due benevolence."* That Greek word for *"due"* is "OPHEILOMENEN." This is a present passive participle. It means *"that which is continuously due, owed, or indebted to someone."* Married love is a continuous *"debt"* that the Christian husband continuously *"owes"* to his wife and that the Christian wife continuously *"owes"* to her husband.

Continuously Owed. Being in the Greek present tense, each is to *"continuously render"* to the other that which is *"continuously due or owed."* There is no letup on this. You can't say when you reach your 5th wedding anniversary "My '*debt*' has been paid off. I no longer '*owe*' this '*debt.*'" You can't say it when you reach your 10th anniversary. You can't say it when you reach your 20th, or 30th, or 50th, or even your 60th or 70th wedding anniversary. This is continuous owing of a continuous debt that will never be paid off until death parts us from our mates. We must never forget this.

No Age Boundaries. There is no boundary or age-group. I know that some of you young people may think that some of us older people are not any longer capable of married love. A couple of young girls were overhearing a conversation that my wife and I were having about two of our friends whom my wife and I introduced to each other. They were each in their 50's when the woman became a widow and the man became a widower and married each other. These young girls were talking and saying the 50-year-old couple were so old. The girls were certain that this couple would not have any kind of married love because they were too old for this. That may be some of your opinions, too, but that if far from the truth. As long as there is life and ability, there is to be married love between Christian husbands and Christian wives. Never forget this. The debt will never be paid until "Digger O'Dell" comes for us and we're buried.

---

h. Continuous Rendering.
The husband is continuously to render what is due to his wife which is here called a *"benevolence."*

Now what is the meaning of that word, *"benevolence"*? The Greek word is EUNOIAN. This is a compound word. EU means *"well."* It is the adverbial form of AGATHOS which means *"good."* NOIAN comes from NOUS which means *"mind."* So this means *"a well or good mind, well affected as far as feelings or emotions are concerned."* The Greek lexicon lists, as one meaning, *"the conjugal duty."*

The husband is to render unto his wife *"the conjugal duty"* (sexual love), and the wife is to render *"the conjugal duty"* (sexual love) unto her husband. It is to be a *"well-minded act."*

Something which is a well affected and a properly understood act. For Christian couples, it is not to be looked at as something that is dirty, filthy, or corrupt. It is blessed of God.

The Debt That Is Owed. So this is what it means when it says, *"Let the husband render unto the wife due benevolence; and likewise also the wife unto the husband."* The debt that is owed. When you are married and you believe as I do, this marriage is for life. It is for keeps. God will never bless me, or any husband, if we turn to a prostitute or another woman for sexual relations. The same goes for my wife or any other wife, if they turn to another man for sexual relations. We, as Christian husbands and Christian wives, are shut up one to

Chapter Three—The Mutuality of a Melodious Marriage

another exclusively. We each have a debt to discharge one to another in regard to the married love relation. There is nobody in this world who is able to pay my wife's debt to me. Only my wife can do this. Likewise, there is nobody in this world who is able to pay my debt to my wife. Only I can do this. We are shut up to each other in this.

Not Like the Unsaved. We are not like the unsaved world, (or even professing Christians not living for the Lord, sad to say) who can go to those other than their mate if the husband or the wife is not interested in fulfilling this marriage obligation. No! We are shut up to each other in this matter. That's why it is incumbent upon us as born-again believers who believe this Book that we follow to the letter, God's Word in this area of married love. We are to *"render due benevolence."*

A Naval Chaplain. When I was a U. S. Naval Chaplain on five years of active duty, I counseled between 3,000 and 4,000 people. I found out that, though it was true, that the husband usually had a greater desire than the wife in this area, it was not at all always the case. Many times the wife was complaining to me that the husband had failed to render to her that which is due to the wife as far as married love is concerned. The husband should render to the wife, and the wife should render to the husband. There is a mutuality here.

> (7:4) *"The wife hath not power of her own body, but the husband: and likewise also the husband hath not power of his own body, but the wife."*

"Hath Not Power." The Greek word for *"hath not power"* is an interesting word. The word for power or authority is EXOUSIA which is a noun. It is the same word as in John 1:12, *"to them gave he power to become the sons of God."*

Here it is from the verb, EXOUSIAZO. Once again it is a present tense in Greek which means a continuous action. It means *"the authority, the rule, the dominion, and the jurisdiction."* What it means is that the wife "continuously," all the time, from the time she says "I do" to her Christian husband that she does not have any *"authority"* over her body. She does not have any *"rule"* over that body. She no longer has any *"dominion"* or *"jurisdiction"* over that body. Her body is now jointly owned by herself and her husband. In this verse, God begins with the wife.

Wives Do Not Rule. In verse 3, God speaks to the husband. But in this verse 4, he starts with the wife. Why? We are not told. The first thing that is mentioned is that the wife is continuously **not** to have *"rule, authority, dominion or jurisdiction"* over her own body. When she was single, her body (in addition to being totally the Lord's--1 Corinthians 6:19) was only hers. But once you are married that all changes. The wife has not continuous *"power and authority"* over that body. Once she is married, her husband now has a share in the *"jurisdiction, rule, dominion, and authority."*

No Exclusive Right. In the last part of verse 4 it says: *"and likewise also the husband hath not power of his own body, but the wife."* Once again, the verb is in the Greek present tense which signifies a progressive and continuous action. The husband does **not** continuously any longer have exclusive *"authority, rule, dominion, or jurisdiction"* over his own body. The wife (in addition to the Lord's total ownership--1 Corinthians 6:19) now owns part of him. You have a mutual ownership of property over each other's body. That's what God is saying here in these verses.

We Are Not Our Own. We are **not** able, if we are Christian couples who are obedient to this verse, to say *"I **am** my own and I'm **not** going to do anything regarding married love with you my husband or my wife."* You **can't** say *"I **am** going to violate verse 3, and I'm **not** going to render due benevolence."* You can't keep the power of your own body. If you do this in your marriage, you are headed for trouble. You will be God's "doghouse," so to speak, and will be disobedient to the Word of God. God will judge your marriage for that.

Age Doesn't Matter. I don't care what your age, or how many years you have been married. We are all headed for trouble if we violate Verses 3 and 4. Notice, once again, these verbs used here are all Greek present tenses. They convey progressive and continuous action.

---

i. A Summary Verse.

Verse 5, I think, sums up what God has talked about in the first 4 verses of the chapter. It wraps up the Bible's teachings on married love into a nice and neat package.

When I was a Naval Chaplain on active duty, I preached the Word of God. I was an evangelist in uniform. I didn't teach a lot of doctrines. You can't do much of this while in the uniform of a Chaplain. You mainly preach the Word in the sense of evangelism, and try to win souls to Christ. This I tried to do. When those in the Navy or the Marines came in for counseling concerning marriage problems, I usually took them to these verses in 1 Corinthians 7:1-5 and told them that this was God's answer to marriage dilemmas. I used these verses even though most of them were not Christians.

People Don't Follow Advice. Of course, I knew, as I was sitting there talking to them, that they would get up and walk out of the office, go their own way, and do exactly what they wanted to do regardless of God's teachings. I still opened up the Bible and showed them these verses. I didn't give them all

Chapter Three—The Mutuality of a Melodious Marriage

the Greek and all the details like I am including here. I told them that this is God's way, and God's will regarding married love. I trust that this will not be the way with those of you who are listening to me now. I trust that you will go out of here and not only **know** what God expects of you in this area, but that you will also **do** what God expects of you.

I hope that you will both **know** and **practice** what God has told us. I have put five numbers in brackets in the following verse because these are the five important elements that we should understand concerning our married love relationships with our Christian mates.

> (7:5) *"Defraud ye not one the other, except it be:*
> [1] *with consent*
> [2] *for a time,*
> [3] *that ye may give yourselves to fasting and prayer: and*
> [4] *come together again,*
> [5] *that Satan tempt you not for your incontinency."*

> **j. The Meaning of *"Defraud."***
> The first observation concerns the Greek verb translated *"defraud."* It is an imperative or a command.

It is also, once again, in the present tense. It's a continuous action. But, notice, it is also a negative command or a prohibition. In the Greek language there are two ways to express negative commands or prohibitions. (1) One is with the present tense negative command, like we have here. (2) The other is with the aorist tense negative command, which we don't have here.

Greek Negative Commands. If it were an aorist tense negative command or prohibition, it would mean *"Don't even **begin** to defraud one another."* You haven't defrauded your mate yet. Don't start defrauding that mate. That is what the aorist prohibition would mean.

Stop an Action. The present tense negative command or prohibition (which we have here represented by the English verb, *"defraud"*) means *"to stop an action already in progress."* It means to quit doing something you are doing. In this case it means to *"stop defrauding one another"* in the married love relationships. All throughout the New Testament we see many present imperative commands which are negative prohibitions. All of these mean to stop an action already in progress. One example would be in **2 Corinthians 6:14**:

"***Be ye not unequally yoked together with unbelievers***: *for what fellowship hath righteousness with unrighteousness? and what communion hath light with darkness?*"

Since the Greek verb translated "be ye not unequally yoked together" is a present tense negative command or prohibition, it means to "*stop being unequally yoked together with unbelievers.*" The Corinthian Christians were being "*unequally yoked together with unbelievers.*" Paul told them to stop doing this.

Present Prohibition. So in 1 Corinthians 7:5, this present prohibition indicates clearly that these Corinthian Christian husbands and wives were defrauding each other in regard to their married love relationship. They were saying "No" to one another and refusing one another in this important area of their marriage. Paul says to quit it and to stop it! It is an action that has already been taking place.

Meaning of "*Defraud*." What does the Greek verb for "*defraud*" mean? The word is "APOSTEREITE." This is a present tense form of the verb, "APOSTEREO." Since it is in the present tense, it signifies a continuous action, as mentioned before. It means "*to deprive one or to debar one from something.*" It is a compound Greek word from APO plus STEREO. STEREO conveys the idea of "*firmness or hardness.*" It is "*an unjust holding of something that is someone else's.*"

---

k. "*Debarring*"

This idea of "*debarring*" is something that my wife takes up in her "HUSBAND-LOVING LESSONS." [BFT #463 @ $16.00+$4.00 S&H]

We discussed this together before she wrote it. She makes an excellent point. It is like building a wall between one another because it speaks of "*debarring, or hardness, and firmness.*" She tells the wives to whom she is speaking: "*Stop building a wall. Stop defrauding. Stop depriving one another of their just due in married love.*" She says the first day the wall is so high. The second day it is a little higher. The next day and the next week it gets higher yet. The wall gets higher and higher and stronger and stronger. It gets firmer and firmer.

Building Walls. She suggests, and I concur with her, that the wall you should build should be between your husband, if you are a wife, and some other man. Build that wall. Christian husbands should not be building a wall between their mates, but between them and another woman. Build that wall tall, strong, and firm. Don't ever smash through it. The force of this "*stop defrauding*" is "*Stop depriving. Stop building strong and firm walls against your mate. Stop defrauding and refusing one another married love.*"

Chapter Three—The Mutuality of a Melodious Marriage

> **I. Exceptions Listed.**
> If you notice in the next part of verse 5 there are a few exceptions.
> *". . . except it be*
> [1] *with consent*
> [2] *for a time,*
> [3] *that ye may give yourselves to fasting and prayer; and*
> [4] *come together again,*
> [5] *that Satan tempt you not for your incontinency."*

(1) *"With consent."* This Greek word for *"consent"* is "SYMPHONOS." It is the same word from which we get our English word, *"symphony."* It is a compound word formed by two smaller Greek words. SYN means *"with."* PHONE means a *"voice or a sound."* Taken together, it means literally *"a voice or sound with one another."* It means *"to harmonize or to sound together."* Don't refuse one another married love unless there is mutual *"consent."* Both parties agree that this will be delayed on this occasion. There must be mutual *"agreement with consent."* If there is not mutual *"consent,"* as far as I interpret this verse, you are to *"stop defrauding"* your mate. You are not to refuse married love unless there is *"consent."*

(2) *"For a time."* Notice also that it says that this mutual *"consent"* is only to be *"for a time."* This Greek word for *"time"* is KAIROS." There is another word for *"time"* which is CHRONOS. That word means chronological time like minutes, years, days, and months. This word is "KAIROS" which is a particular season. It means a limited period of time. It is not forever and a day. This refusal of married love, even with *"consent,"* is not to be for an extended period of time. It is just to be for a limited amount of CHRONOS time.

(3) *"That ye may give yourselves."* We also see that this mutual *"consent"* *"for a time"* must be for a proper purpose. The purpose suggested here is *"that ye may give yourselves to fasting and prayer."* There must be a proper and sufficient reason for this defrauding, refusal, and depriving one another of married love. Fasting is doing without food. We know what prayer is. This Greek word for *"give yourselves"* is SCHOLAZETE from "SCHOLAZO." We get the word, *"scholarship"* and *"scholar"* from this. It is in the present tense again and therefore refers to a continuous action. It means *"to be at leisure."* A scholar is one who has SCHOLE. He is *"at leisure"* and can devote himself entirely to study.

> **m. Rules For Depriving.**
> If you continue to say "No" in married love, continue to defraud, and continue to deprive your spouse of married love without following God's rules here, this is sin.

> This discontinuation of married love must be accompanied by
>   (1) mutual consent,
>   (2) only for a time, and
>   (3) only for a good and valid purpose so that you may continuously give yourselves to something else.

The two reasons given in verse 5 are examples of good purposes and reasons for abstaining from married love. There may be other reasons such as prior to a birth of a baby, illness, or separation due to work that may be acceptable, but here are at least two spiritual reasons.

    (4) "*Come together again.*" The next part of verse 5 says, "*. . . and come together again, . . .*" When should this "again" take place? Someone might wonder about how long a "*season*" is meant by "*for a season.*" Whatever is meant by the length of time referred to in this "*season,*" when this mutual "*consent*" which is only "*for a season*" and for a good reason at that point God commands you as married Christians to "*come together again*" and resume your married love relations as husband and wife.

    Meaning of "Season." I believe the length of this "*season*" of time is indicated partially right here in verse 5. The two valid purposes for abstaining from married love given in this verse are either (1) "*fasting*" or (2) "*prayer.*"

    "***Prayer.***" Speaking of "*prayer,*" how long do you pray? Not very long, if you are honest with yourself. So, according to this verse, you can give yourself over to earnest praying and then, when this urgent prayer need is over, you are commanded to "*come together again.*" You can, perhaps, have a few days of prayer. But the duration of time indicated is linked to how long your prayer lasts. Most of us, and probably most people in Paul's day, did not continually give themselves in prayer for any long-extended days or weeks.

    "***Fasting.***" The second indication of time is the word, "*fasting,*" which means to go without solid food. How long do people normally do that? How many meals did you have today? How many snacks did you have today? You can go without solid food for a few days, but that is usually the extent of it. The "*season*" of time is implied right in the context. The point is that God's Word teaches us in this verse that there is a time element involved in this abstinence. We're to have this agreement of mutual "*consent*" only "*for a season*" so that

Chapter Three—The Mutuality of a Melodious Marriage

we can give ourselves to a spiritual exercise of prayer or fasting or some other equally proper purpose, and then husbands and wives are to reestablish their married love.

"*Come Together Again.*" This Greek verb for "*come together again*" is also in the present tense. It is SUNERCHESTHE. As in the other verbs in this section, this is the present tense of SUNERCHO. The present tense indicates a continuous and constant action in this regard. The verb means, according to the Greek lexicon, "*to come together with one another jointly, or to cohabit matrimonially.*" This is technical language for the marriage relationship.

Military Exceptions. I believe there is a time-frame that is required by God and we go against God's Word and His will if we do not honor God's standards and plan. I realize that some of you can make all kinds of excuses as to why this time frame is not for you. There may be extenuating circumstances. For example, I was stationed for 12 months with the U. S. Marines in Okinawa while I was on active duty as a Naval Chaplain corps. No Marine or Navy wives were allowed to go with their husbands at that time. My wife was in Miami, Florida during that year where we lived during my last duty station. We were apart for one year. Though this is not normal for married couples to be apart for one year, that was the fact. You might have some sickness or other things that would be extenuating circumstances to extend this "*season*" beyond the normal limits.

> **n.** "*That Satan tempt you not.*"
> **But we must be very careful in these matters because of the next clause in this verse 5, "*that Satan tempt you not for your incontinency.*"**

This "*coming together again*" is a continuous present action. You must continually come together again and establish your married love relations. If you do not do that, Satan is in a position to "*tempt you.*" because of "*your incontinency.*" That Greek verb for "*tempt*" is PEIRAZO. It is a present tense verb once again. It signifies a continuous action. Satan is always ready to test and to tempt the husband and wife as long as they fail to follow the requirements that God has given us in this verse. This Greek verb for "*tempt*" means "*to test in either a good intent or an evil intent.*" Though it is a neutral word, the context makes clear what is meant. In this case, Satan is doing this "*tempting*" with a very evil intent. He desires to trip you up and then point his accusing finger of guilt at you. This is what he does.

"*Incontinency.*" If we fail to follow God's rules here in these verses, Satan will "*tempt*" the husband and he will "*tempt*" the wife because of their "*incontinency.*" The Greek word for that term is AKRASIAN. "A" is a negative prefix meaning, "*no.*" KRASIAN means "*power or control.*" Both parts of the word taken together, AKRASIAN, means that there is *"no power, or no self control."* This *"no self-control"* condition is what the husband puts his wife in if he deprives his wife of married love. By the same token, this *"no self-control"* condition is what the wife puts her husband in if she deprives him of married love. Unless each and every one of the preceding four requirements are accepted and followed by both husband and wife, they deprive each other of *"self-control"* in this very powerful emotion. This is what *"incontinency"* means.

---
o. No Adultery--Regardless.
Remember this, however, no matter what the husband or wife does or doesn't do, there is absolutely no excuse whatsoever for either party to commit adultery.

When either the husband or the wife fails to follow these verses, it is a terrible sin against the mate. Because of this failure, suppose the husband is tempted and commits adultery. Though the wife did not commit the adultery, she might be partially to blame because of her actions and inactions as a wife. But her refusal is absolutely no excuse for his adultery. He is responsible for his own personal purity!

Failure Is Dangerous. Because of this failure, suppose the wife is tempted and commits adultery. Though the husband did not commit the adultery, he might be partially to blame because of his actions and inactions as a husband. The wife might be tempted to commit adultery with someone with whom she is working in the office--and this is how it sometimes starts. But his refusal is absolutely no excuse for her adultery. She is responsible for her own personal purity!

The Bakker Case. The world has made a joke about Jim Bakker and his sin. They have called it a "Bakker's dozen." By the time you count all of the prostitutes and others maybe it does add up to that many. One of the papers wrote that his former wife, Tammy, shut this man out of her bedroom prior to this happening for many, many months. This does not excuse Bakker for committing adultery, but Tammy was wrong. It is interesting in the light of this verse and the exegesis of it. Satan did "tempt" him. He may have been tempted a long time before this, I don't know.

---
p. Marriage Break-Ups.
I would imagine that in marriage break-ups or adulterous relationships in marriages, either by the husband or the wife, there is much alleged self-righteousness on the part of both parties.

There is talk about the "innocent party." At Dallas Theological Seminary we were taught that the so-called "innocent party" can divorce and re-marry. In most cases, I don't think that there is a 100% "innocent party." Sometimes there may be, but in most cases I don't believe that there is. If divorce does take place, I believe the Scriptures teach that the remaining husband or wife must be restored to their mate, or remain single until the death of the mate. This is taught in 1 Corinthians 7, Romans 7, the Gospel of Mark, and the Gospel of Luke. We must be careful to follow carefully God's Word in the matter of married love, lest Satan's master stroke of "temptation" and marriage disaster eventuates.

● **2. THE SUPPLICATIONS:**
(1 Peter 3:7) *"Likewise, ye husbands, dwell with them according to knowledge, giving honour unto the wife, as unto the weaker vessel, and as being heirs together of the grace of life; that your PRAYERS be not hindered."*

> **a. Mutual Prayer.**
> **A second thing that Christian husbands and Christian wives should do mutually is to participate in supplications and mutual *"prayers."* These *"prayers"* should not be *"hindered."***

If Satan is tempting either the husband or the wife or both in this area of a lack of sexual control because 1 Corinthians 7:1-5 is not being followed, other things will also happen. The joint prayer life will cease. The couple will tend to get irritated with each other and argue about tiny things, including money matters.

> **b. Bitterness Enters.**
> **If the wife that has refused her husband what is his, his marital due, his part-authority, part-rule, part-dominion, and part-jurisdiction over his wife's body, that makes him angry. That makes him bitter.**

That makes him out-of-sorts, and cantankerous. Or, on the other hand, if the husband refuses the wife what is her part-authority, part-rule, part-dominion, or part-jurisdiction over her husband's body, that makes her angry. That makes her bitter. That makes her out-of-sorts and cantankerous. That makes the wall between husband and wife get built higher and higher as well as stronger and stronger.

> **c. Satan's Tempting.**
> Cantankerousness and bickering back and forth is the result of Satan's tempting you for lack of control. It is not only your lack of control in the sexual aspect, but also, quite often, a lack of control as far as your temper is concerned.

If you don't believe this happens, just look at your marriage in the past, in the present, and perhaps into the future. I hope this is not the case too often. We must recognize that this might be another avenue that Satan uses to break up homes. We must have prayers jointly together and they must not be hindered because of these things. We must read mutually the Word of God, and this can not be done if there is not a mutual understanding of one another or a mutual married love relationship and understanding between husband and wife.

- ### 3. THE SENSITIVITY:
    (Ephesians 4:32): *"And be ye kind one to another, tenderhearted, FORGIVING one another, even as God for Christ's sake hath forgiven you."*

> **Forgiveness must be practiced.**

Paul is talking to Christians generally, but I think that we can apply this to husbands and wives. If we are Christians, we should be kind in the home. That is mutuality. The longer we do not forgive our mate the longer the antipathy, the anger, and everything else will be built up. You know this. It must be practiced on a daily basis so that God can bless our homes.

- ### 4. THE STEADFASTNESS:
    (1 Corinthians 4:2) *"Moreover it is required in stewards, that a man be found FAITHFUL."*

> **We must be STEADFAST and FAITHFUL in our marriage vows and obligations throughout our marriages.**

A Stewardship. Marriage is a stewardship, and we are stewards of what God has given us. We ought to be faithful in that marriage. Faithfulness is one of the things that should be practiced throughout our lifetime together. We must be faithful in the marriage vows, faithful in the marriage bed, faithful in married love, faithful in loyalties, faithful in helpfulness, and faithful in all these other matters that enter into being *"one flesh."* I have 16 words that I want to touch on briefly for mutuality in a marriage. These are for the managers of a "melodious marriage."

5. OTHER SENTIMENTS:

a. <u>Sincerity</u>. Let's be sincere one with another. Let's not have lies and half truths and deception. When we don't feel good, let's tell our spouse. So many people cover-up and are insincere, gooey, and mushy. You might do that (though you shouldn't) to your friends, but don't do it to your husband or your wife. We know our spouses better then that.

b. <u>Silence</u>. Many times silence is golden, as they say. Sometimes it is yellow, I realize, but many times it is golden. Often you should just be silent and shut your mouth. Don't argue or bicker. Don't say a word. The Lord knew all about this. In the book of Revelation, He said, *"There was silence in Heaven about the space of half an hour"* (Revelation 8:1a).

c. <u>Sentimentality</u>. You might only be taking your wife to a candle-light dinner at a Bible camp, where you don't even have washing facilities in your own cabin, but you have sentimentality none the less. This is great. Let's not forget it. I am sure I lack sentimentality more than anything else as far as flowers, cards, and gifts are concerned. My wife is the sentimental one, and I'm thankful for that. We've been married since 1948, but I seem to require still more time to work on this marital virtue.

d. <u>Sociability</u>. Be sociable one with another. Be sociable with others as well. Learn how to relate properly and as a Christian.

e. <u>Sparkle</u>. You need to shine. Don't be glum as if you have lost your best friend. Don't let people know that you are not recently married. When my wife and I go out to eat, and we see a couple, we might say to each other *"No, they are not married. They are too happy."* Have you ever observed people. Sometimes you can see couples that have a certain sparkle. Let people think that you are newly married. Have a sparkle about you when you are together. Keep the love-light burning.

f. <u>Stability</u>. Be stable. Husband, try to be stable. Wife, try to be stable. Try to stay to the Word of God. Don't drift away from God's truths found in His Book.

g. <u>Self Respect</u>. Have it. Keep it. Use It. Respect one another. It is so needful in marriage.

h. <u>Softness</u>. This is in the sense of tenderness. It is easy to be hard and harsh. Rather, be soft and tender in the right sense of the word.

I. <u>Sweethearts</u>. Always be sweethearts. I notice that one of my wife's titles (she has interesting titles in her *Husband-Loving Lessons*) is "Home, Sweetheart, Home," instead of "home sweet home." Husband, be glad to see her when you come home from where ever you have been. Wife, be glad to see him even though both of you may have worked hard all day.

j. Stubbornness. Be careful about being stubborn. Yes, we want to hold on to our solid Biblical values and standards, but in simple matters of living, let's refuse to be stubborn. Husbands, let's listen to our mate's ideas, and accept them if they are sound, even though they might differ from ours.

k. Support. Support one another. Husbands, we are to support our wives. We are to take care of them. We are to prop each other up

l. Strife. May it not be named among us. It is so easy to get into, isn't it. Perhaps you haven't eaten. You are hungry, tired, and irritable. In such conditions, strife often enters in. Keep it away. Keep your blood sugar up.

m. Sympathy. We must use sympathy toward our mate. When they are upset or sick, we cannot disregard their condition. Our sympathy can often make things better.

n. Suffering.

Sickness and Health. I suppose the closest and most precious marriage melody is played when one of the mate is a suffering mate if the other one is concerned and sympathetic. The marriage vows that we take, and I trust that we believe them, mention the words, *"in sickness and in health."* As we look down the corridor of time many of us don't look forward to sickness. We don't expect it. We only look forward to health, but sickness is often present.

The Marriage Ceremony. When I marry couples I still say *"in sickness and in health."* To have that mate who is healthy to stay with that one who is in bad health for weeks, months, or years, takes grace and care. I had cancer in my body. I had Hodgkin's Disease which is cancer of the lymph glands. My neck was puffed up very decidedly in January to July of 1985. I took laetrile, but it didn't seem to help very much. The cancer kept on growing. Then I took the conventional treatment, chemotherapy. In this case, together with the laetrile and the Lord's hand, it worked and the swelling went down remarkably. The Lord used it and I am in remission. I began by going every 3 months to the cancer doctor. Presently I go only once a year. He examines me and tells me I'm all right for now. As of this book printing, I have been well from that cancer for 15 years. Thank the Lord for these added days of service for Him.

Recovering From Cancer. During those long months of recovery from this cancer, I had some suffering, and my wife stood by me. She took me to my chemotherapy treatments. They are terrible treatments. I don't know how many months or days the Lord will give me, but I'm seeking to be especially faithful to Him in the days, weeks, months, or years that He gives me. I'm not going to stop preaching or teaching the Word of God. I'm not going to stop being faithful to the things of the Lord. Often times, when one mate is laid aside due to suffering, the other mate deserts that one and says the marriage is over. During illness, distress, death, or financial loss is when we need each other the most.

Chapter Three—The Mutuality of a Melodious Marriage 57

o. **Speech.**
Be careful! I'm a speech teacher and have been for many years. I have my Ph.D. in speech. The Scripture says that we are to have *"sound speech, that cannot be condemned"* (Titus 2:8). Let's take care of our speech one to another, so it is not harsh. So often it is easy to have speech that cuts and hurts. If you have been married very long you know exactly how to do it. Even if you have only been married a short time you know how to make your speech that is the sharpest that will hurt your mate the most. It is a terrible, and a sinful thing to do, but we know just what to say to make the other one mad. We must be careful of our speech.

p. **Serenity.** This is a wonderful thing. It is peace which is *"Shalom"* in Hebrew. IRENE in the Greek. That is where we get the name Irene. May there be serenity in our homes so that the Lord will bless these homes for His glory.

Chapter Four
The Multiplication of a Melodious Marriage

The last three chapters discussed "THE **MAKER** OF A MELODIOUS MARRIAGE," "THE **MANAGERS** OF A MELODIOUS MARRIAGE," and "THE **MUTUALITY** OF A MELODIOUS MARRIAGE." This chapter discusses "THE **MULTIPLICATION** OF A MELODIOUS MARRIAGE."

Importance of Future Generations. I hope that some of you could take these principles that we have learned from God's Word (they are not my principles, but God's principles) and multiply them by sharing with friends of yours who need this teaching. I am particularly anxious about your children and your grandchildren that they will be able to multiply in their home a "melodious marriage" with all the Christian graces that go with it. It is not enough to have moms and dads to know what the Lord's work is all about and to have a right kind of home with Christian standards. This "melodious marriage" must be passed on to our children and to our grandchildren.

Our Children. I told you before that I have four sons and one daughter. Aside from our second son, Dave, (born in 1951) who has mental illness, our children have been a delight to our hearts. Dave is a delight, but he is also a great burden as you can imagine. We pray and ask the Lord to help him even in this condition.

Our oldest son. Don Jr. was born in 1949. He is married to Jeanette. They have two children, Elizabeth and Rebecca. Our third son, Dick, was born in 1954. He is married to Lorraine. They have three children, Richard, Jacob, and Jonathan. Our fourth son, Dan, was born in 1965. They have one child, Anna. These sons follow the Word of God. They are a blessing to me. Their wives also are a blessing to all of us.

Our Girl. Our daughter, who lives in Jacksonville, Florida, is Dianne. She was born in 1956. (We have all "D's" Don, Dave, Dick, Dianne, and Dan.) Dianne is married to Reggie. They have two children, Kristen and Megan. Dianne reads the Bible and is a blessing to me. Reggie is also a blessing to all of us.

Our Youngest Son. Dan, our youngest son is presently helping me full-time as Assistant to the Director of the Bible For Today. He is also my Assistant Pastor of the 𝕭𝖎𝖇𝖑𝖊 𝕱𝖔𝖗 𝕿𝖔𝖉𝖆𝖞 𝕭𝖆𝖕𝖙𝖎𝖘𝖙 𝕮𝖍𝖚𝖗𝖈𝖍. I am happy that our family has been blessed of God.

Grandchildren. I am always praying for our grandchildren. What is there in life that we have as parents but the raising of our own children with hopes that they will raise their children in the things of our Saviour. What is our mission? We must hold the line of Scriptural truth: our belief in the Bible as the inerrant Word of God, the Deity of Christ, His bodily resurrection, His blood atonement, and all of the doctrines that we hold dear. These must be multiplied in our families. They must be duplicated. We have to teach others also as it says in 2 Timothy.

2 Timothy 2:2
*And **the things that thou hast heard** of me among many witnesses, the same **commit thou to faithful men, who shall be able to teach others also**.*

I am concerned also about multiplication of our position. We need to multiply ourselves and our beliefs for the next generation. This is very important otherwise we will die out. In order to have a "**MELODIOUS MARRIAGE**," we must have our CHILDREN in proper order. This will enable us also to MULTIPLY the concepts of "**MELODIOUS MARRIAGE**" for future generations as well.

A. Parents' Duties Regarding their Children:

● 1. THE STRESS:

(Ephesians 6:4a) "*And ye fathers, provoke not your children to wrath:...*"

---

a. The Meaning of "*Provoke to wrath.*"

It is translated from the Greek word, PARORGIZETE. It is in the present tense. It is a prohibition or a negative command. As mentioned before, in the Greek language, a present tense prohibition signifies to STOP an action already in progress. God commands "*fathers*" or "*parents*" to STOP provoking their "*children to wrath.*" The verb means literally "*to anger alongside.*" Therefore, "*to enrage; anger; or to provoke to wrath.*"

Chapter Four—Multiplication of a Melodious Marriage

> **b. The Duties of "*Fathers*."**
> That word for "*fathers*" could also refer to "*parents*" meaning either fathers or mothers. Since this is a present tense prohibition, it implies that the "fathers" or "parents" in the Ephesus church were "*provoking their children to wrath.*"

Stressful Conditions. Because of this, there were stressful conditions in the homes. You might ask, "*How can you discipline your child without provoking them to wrath and thus violating this verse?*" The answer to that question is that you must start early in the child's life. There must be a fair, proper, consistent, and Scriptural discipline from early childhood. If this has taken place, you will not have this "*provoking to wrath.*" The child's will must be trained to do the right thing at the right time. When Dad or Mom discipline that child, they will no longer have a wrathful reaction to discipline. They will say, in effect, "*Yes I did wrong. I deserve punishment. Therefore I am not going to have a wrathful reaction.*" I believe that this is one of the solutions and answers.

When Should Spanking Begin? I was asked this morning, "*When do you first begin the physical spanking or discipline of your child?*" My answer was that you should begin proper discipline of your child as soon as you detect his or her a rebelliousness in word, deed, or attitude. Whether it is spitting out food or being willful in other ways. You parents can detect such an improper spirit. As soon as they have rebellion of proper authority, there should be a proportionate use, however slight, of physical discipline. Don't hurt or injure the child, but he or she should get the message. The child should get the picture that this is not in line with what you expect as a parent. The message has gotten across with the least amount of force necessary to accomplish the mission. This is always the rule.

> **c. Philadelphia Schools.**
> When I taught in the Philadelphia school system we had a rule that we could not use corporal punishment, but we could use self-defensive measures.

There are five areas where we can use force against a pupil. I looked up these in the applicable statute book because I needed to know what I could or couldn't do.

> **Five Permitted Areas of Force**
> 1. To break up a fight or quell a disturbance.
> 2. To protect property.
> 3. To prevent someone trying to injure another child.
> 4. To remove drugs or weapons from a child.
> 5. To use self-defense.

<u>Self-Defense</u>. When a student approached me and I told them to stay away; or if I were trying to keep a student in the room if they had a detention; or if a student came and touched me to try to push me away; that is when I was permitted to retaliate with physical force. If I had to punch or push, I still had to use only the minimum force necessary to defend myself and accomplish the task.

<u>Be Careful</u>. Some teachers told me that I shouldn't have put myself in that position. I knew the laws of Pennsylvania. The school law may say no physical force, but the state law says that you can use physical force in self-defense or for any of the above situations. To me, that is self-defense if someone comes up to me and just touches me.

● **2. THE SUPERVISION:**

> Ephesians (6:4b) *". . . but bring them up . . ."*
> *"bring up"* is the translation of the Greek word, EKTREPHETE. It means *"to rear up to maturity; to cherish; or train; to bring up or nourish."*

<u>Supervise the Children</u>. We are to supervise our children. This is again in the Greek present tense. It is to be a continuous action. We are to continue to *"bring them up."* Never cease *"bringing them up"* in a good way, supervising them, and making sure that they know the right path of the Word of God. Never give up on them. Don't say, *"Well, I've tried for one year and that little child is so bad. I'm just going to give up."* Continue to supervise. Continue to rear up. Continue to *"bring them up"* to maturity and prepare them for the day that they will leave the shelter of your roof.

Chapter Four—Multiplication of a Melodious Marriage

Under the Roof. When your roof is over your children's head they are responsible to you to do as the rules of the home dictate. When they are away from your home and out from under your roof, then they are responsible before God to perform the duties that they would think are wise and prudent. But as long as they are under the roof and eating Dad's and Mom's food, they must follow the rules of the house. They are to be supervised until they reach maturity.

● **3. THE SPANKING:**

> Ephesians (6:4c) "... *in the nurture* ..."
> "*Nurture*" is the translation of the Greek word, PAIDEIA. It implies "*child-training and discipline, including spanking as needed.*"

When Spanking Stops. Spanking usually stops at a younger age. I would hope that you don't have to continue the spanking and the "nurturing" beyond a certain age. Sometimes the older ones need a little bit of assistance along these lines. PAIDEIA, in addition to other things, has to do with such things as training with corporal punishment or spanking as necessary. I have always used four rules to govern the discipline of my children as they were growing up.

Four Rules When Disciplining
1. Only--when they need it. Never when not needed.
2. Always--when they need it. Never pass it up when needed.
3. Proper discipline. The right kind and the right attitude.
4. Sufficient discipline. The right amount, neither too little or too much.

Minimum Force Necessary. What I am saying in regard to the discipline of your child is that you should use the minimum force needed to accomplish proper and wise discipline at the age when your child shows signs of rebellion. Start early enough with this discipline so that you will not "*provoke your child to wrath.*" There are a number of verses in the book of Proverbs that deal with the discipline of our children.

✔ **Proverbs 3:12**
  "For **whom the LORD loveth he correcteth; even as a father the son** *in whom* **he delighteth.**"
✔ **Proverbs 13:24**
  "He that spareth his rod hateth his son: but **he that loveth him chasteneth him betimes.**" "*Betimes*" means "*early.*"

✔ Proverbs 19:18
"**Chasten thy son while there is hope**, and let not thy soul spare for his crying."
✔ Proverbs 22:6
"**Train up a child in the way he should go**: and when he is old, he will not depart from it."
✔ Proverbs 22:15
"**Foolishness *is* bound in the heart of a child; *but* the rod of correction shall drive it far from him.**"
✔ Proverbs 23:13-14
"**Withhold not correction from the child**: for *if* thou beatest him with the rod, he shall not die. Thou shalt beat him with the rod, and **shalt deliver his soul from hell.**"
✔ Proverbs 29:15
"The rod and reproof give wisdom: but **a child left *to himself* bringeth his mother to shame.**"
✔ Proverbs 29:17
"**Correct thy son, and he shall give thee rest**; yea, he shall give delight unto thy soul."

Eight Proverbs of Counsel. These are all Proverbs. There are eight verses here which are standard verses for child training and child discipline in order that we may have a "melodious marriage." A *"child left to himself"* and out of line brings to the home that used to be melodious and harmonious, off-beat and off-key cacophony (bad sounds.) You might say everything was going well until junior came along.

Avoid Discord. Unless we train-up our children correctly we will have discord. We start out with a solo in the musical rendition of life. Then we are married and it becomes a duet. Then the child comes and it becomes a trio. Then a quartet. Then a quintet. Then a sextet, or however many children the Lord gives to us. If each of these children are not in line and in harmony with the Word of God, the marriage will not be any longer melodious. There will be fighting and bickering in the home about how to raise the children. There must be unity to make that marriage melodious.

● **4. THE SPEAKING:**

Ephesians (6:4d) "... *and admonition of the Lord.*"
"Admonition" is the translation of the Greek word, NOUTHESIA. It means, literally, *"putting into mind."* It includes speaking and reasoning with your children. This can be done more effectively with an older child, perhaps, though it can be used even with little children.

Chapter Four—Multiplication of a Melodious Marriage 65

When Do Explanations Come? It isn't always necessary when the little one asks *"Why?"* to discuss it at that time. The main thing is to have the child do what they are told immediately and without question. The questions can come **after** the obedience has been performed. Obedience has been defined as *"Doing what is wanted when it's wanted."* That is obedience. Notice the two significant words in this definition: (1) *"what,"* and (2) *"when."* Doing what is wanted at a time other than when it is wanted is not obedience. Doing immediately what is not wanted is not obedience. It must be **what** you ask the child to do **when** you ask him to do it.

Wait Until After. Sometimes, after the child does what he or she is told, we can tell them the reason for our order and talk to them about it if we want to. I have nothing against this. But God wants us to bring our children up not only in the *"nurture,"* but also in the *"admonition of the Lord."* The *"admonition"* involves our speaking to our children. This *"admonition"* must be *"of the Lord."* It involves showing them from the Word of God why certain things are not right and dishonoring to the Lord and to His Word.

● **5. THE SPARING:**
(Proverbs 13:24) *"He that SPARETH HIS ROD hateth his son: but he that loveth him chasteneth him betimes."* (early)

Meaning of *"Betimes.*" *"Betimes"* is an old English word meaning *"early."* Discipline must begin early in the child's life. The *"rod"* is an implement in order to physically discipline our children. This Hebrew word is used of a *"club used as a shepherd's implement."* The *"sparing"* of that *"rod"* means the disuse of corporal discipline of our children, when they need it and only when they need it. According to this verse, when you *"spare"* that *"rod,"* it shows that you hate your son or daughter. Love is reflected in proper *"chastening"* of your children. You must, as they say, *"apply the board of education to the seat of learning."*

Sparing And Hating. You *"hate"* your child if you *"spare"* the rod because, without it, your children will grow up like Topsy. No one will care about them. They are going to grow up like weeds, without care, instead of beautiful plants and flowers that gives fragrance to other lives.

Incident of Nonsense. When I was teaching in the Philadelphia School system, I was dealing with a boy in school that was mean and out-of-sorts in his actions. I didn't put up with nonsense in my class. We had a very permissive principal, so if there is any discipline at all, it had to take place within the four walls where I taught. This boy's father came down to talk to me about things. This boy called me everything from soup to nuts. He had a very loud and disrespectful mouth. The father came in. We met with the father, the vice principal and the boy. The father said "I understand my boy said so and so to you." I said *"That's right."* The father told the boy, *"If you ever again address your teacher in that manner, I am going to mop the floor up with you."* Then he turned to me and said I never laid a hand on my son. He asked his son if that was right and the son agreed. This boy was in junior high school and the dad finally remembered one time that he spanked his boy. I thought to myself, *"That explains it!"* I was appreciative of the father's support, even at this late date, but why did the father wait so long to chasten his son?

Love and Chastening. God says, *"he that loveth him chasteneth him betimes* [or early]." Some parents are afraid of their children. It is a sad thing when the parents are this way. Some teachers are afraid of the children that they teach. The children know that, so they just walk all over the poor teachers. This was especially true in the inner-city of Philadelphia. It's a war zone.

"Combat Pay." While teaching in Philadelphia, I got "combat pay," so to speak, which I put into my Bible for Today ministry so I could serve the Lord which is my prime interest. The school teaching put bread on my table because the Bible For Today ministry was not self-supporting. It was a good tent-making ministry. It was good because I could be home every day at 3:30 and off duty for 2 months during the summer. It was good if you were able to stand it. A teacher must have a cast-iron stomach and a "command-presence" whereby the students know what you mean and want. He has to mean what he says and say what he means.

Make Up Your Mind. Whenever I sent a child from my room to the Dean's office I never gave them another chance. I never changed my mind. I made up my mind. I gave them opportunities to change when they were doing their out-of-line actions. But once I made up my mind, I said *"Out!"* I gave them the proper note and they were out. They begged to stay in the room, but after a while they knew it would do no good. I had to mean what I said and say what I meant.

- **6. THE SPOILING:**
    (Proverbs 19:18) *"CHASTEN thy son while there is hope, and let not thy soul spare for his crying."*

The spoiling of the son is a terrible thing. We're to chasten him before he gets out of hand. Sometimes they cry ahead of time even before they get spanked. But God says, *". . . let not thy soul spare for his crying."*

- **7 . THE STUPIDITY:**
    (Proverbs 22:15): *"FOOLISHNESS is bound in the heart of a child; but the rod of correction shall drive it far from him."*

Proper discipline does "drive" away the child's *"foolishness"* and the various things that he is doing wrong. The child doesn't know life. The parent knows much more about life because he or she has lived longer than that child. No matter how young a parent you may be, you know more than that boy or girl. Remember the *"rod of correction"* will drive foolishness far from a child.

- **8. THE SALVATION:**
    (Proverbs 23:13-14) (23:13) "*Withhold not correction from the child: for if thou beatest him with the rod, he shall not die. (23:14) Thou shalt beat him with the rod, and shalt DELIVER HIS SOUL FROM HELL.*"
    Meaning of "*Beat*." I don't believe that this word "*beat*" is in the wrong sense of beating. One of the meanings of the Hebrew word is "*chastise*" as it is used here. It does not mean what our modern word, "beat," means. One of the meanings given is "*spank*" as it is used here. It doesn't mean somebody beating up someone. It is a discipline that is done with a proper means and method. Salvation is important. How that child behaves to Mom and Dad is how that child might behave to God and to his Word. We will "deliver his soul from Hell" if we have a love for that young one and spank him appropriately-- only when he needs it, but always when he needs it.
- **9. THE SHAME:**
    (Proverbs 29:15) "*The rod and reproof give wisdom: but a child left to himself bringeth his mother to SHAME.*"
    Meaning of "*Rod*." The "*rod*" stands for corporal discipline. "*Reproof*" is the "*admonition*" mentioned earlier. It involves our speaking to our children.

Two Opposite Words to Grasp
"rod" --corporal punishment
"reproof"--admonition, speaking

Some little children seem always to be out-of-sorts. There are some children that you can tell have never had any home-training by the way of discipline. I'm sure that when that mother has to take that little one out, there is some shame involved. It does bring a "*mother to shame*" unless she uses both the "*rod*" and the "*reproof*" to give the child the "*wisdom*" that he needs.

A Shameful Child. A child left completely to himself, just like this young boy I was telling you about, does bring his mother to shame. I think that is why some of the junior high school children that I taught in Philadelphia were such behavior problems. We had a maximum of 33 in a class. We had to teach 5 classes each day, so we had about 150 students a day. Most of them must had "*ashamed*" mothers because they appear to me, as a teacher who knows the principles of the Word of God, that they had been "*left to themselves.*" When the students came to school after each weekend at home, it took me all of Monday and part of Tuesday to get them back in order. When they had been home for a vacation it took several extra days to get them in shape.

Getting Students In Shape. When the students arrived the first of September, at the beginning of the school year, it took weeks to get them in shape. The first day of school they were always angels. You could always see the one who would break out of the angelic heaven and become the devil. That one usually was the one who would give the teacher the most trouble all year. They were children who had been "left to themselves." It is a sad thing. I think they appreciated the firm discipline that I gave them. When I wasn't firm with them, they wondered what was the matter. They appreciated and needed care.

● **10. THE SERENITY:**

(Proverbs 29:17) *"Correct thy son, and he shall give thee REST; yea, he shall give DELIGHT unto thy soul."*

Delight to the Soul. That is a wonderful thing. You look back on the correction, discipline, and training that you gave your sons and your daughters and you can say *"Praise the Lord! What rest that child has given to me because I have been faithful in correcting him and bringing him up in the nurture and admonition of the Lord."* They do give delight after they have been *"corrected"* properly in a Biblical manner.

Great Grief. Those parents who had not been as fortunate as we, have children that did not turn out as ours have. It must give the parents great grief. We know some of these parents, and it is discouraging. I don't know what to say to them. All I can do is pray for them. I know many couples who do not know the multiplication of a "melodious marriage" in their children. I know some pastors who kept their children in line while they were in their home. That is good. But those children are grown up and have moved out of the home. They are now living for the world and the devil. They married unsaved mates and so on. You don't know what went wrong, but it is a sad thing to see this situation. It brings great grief to the parents and grandparents when this happens.

Practical Verses. The verses from Proverbs, dealing with the sparing, the spoiling, the stupidity the salvation, the shame, and the serenity are very practical. They teach us that discipline and chastisement of children is taught in the Bible and we must perform it and hold to it as Christian parents.

B. Examples of Bringing up Children in the Bible:

● 1. SAD EXAMPLES OF BRINGING UP CHILDREN:

> a. The Slaying--Eli's Sons.

(1 Samuel 2:12, 17, 22-25, 29, 34; 4:11) (2:12) *"Now the sons of Eli were sons of Belial; they knew not the Lord.* (2:17) *Wherefore the sin of the young men was very great before the Lord: for men abhorred the offering of the Lord.* (2:22) *Now Eli was very old, and heard all that his sons did unto all Israel; and how they lay with the women that assembled at the door of the tabernacle of the congregation.* (2:23) *And he said unto them, Why do ye such things? for I hear of your evil dealings by all this people.* (2:24) *Nay, my sons; for it is no good report that I hear: ye make the LORD's people to transgress.* (2:25b) *. . . Notwithstanding they hearkened not unto the voice of their father, because the LORD WOULD SLAY THEM. . .* (2:29) *Wherefore kick ye at my sacrifice and at mine offering, which I have commanded in my habitation; and honourest thy sons above me, to make yourselves fat with the chiefest of all the offerings of Israel my people? . . .* (2:34) *And this shall be a sign unto thee, that shall come upon thy two sons, on Hophni and Phinehas; in one day they shall die both of them.* (4:11) *And the ark of God was taken; and the two sons of Eli, Hophni and Phinehas, were slain."*

Eli, a Poor Father. Eli was a priest of God. He should have known how to raise his sons in a proper manner. Maybe he was spending too much time at the tabernacle and not enough time at home. Pastors do this sometimes. When this happens, their families are neglected. Sometimes people who are not pastors get too busy in their work and other activities. They can make a shambles of their home as well. So, the dangers of Eli and his sons are a potential danger for all of us. The sons of Eli were the sons of Belial. That was the devil's crowd. It was Baal worship. Can you imagine that the sons of Eli, the priest of God, did not even know the Lord?

It says in Scripture,
"For what shall it profit a man, if he shall gain the whole world, and lose his own soul?" (Mark 8:36)

What Profit? What would it profit a priest if he gains all the people of Israel to whom he ministers, but loses his own family? What shall it profit a pastor? What shall it profit a dad or mom if they gain all the notoriety, all the money, or all the fame if they lose their own children? That is a sad thing. No multiplication of a "melodious marriage." There is only disharmony and evil.

Nature of Sin. Sin is always *"before the Lord,"* not before men and their standards. Men will sometimes pat you on the back when you sin. God says it's sin and it's in His Book as sin. God's standards must be our standards. Eli's sons didn't care about the sacred offerings of the Lord. These sons were so bad they were committing either fornication or adultery with the women who came to the *"tabernacle."*

Temple Prostitution. This wickedness is similar to what went on in the temples of Baal where they practiced temple prostitution as a part of their "worship" of Baal. The men gave their money to have sex with either a prostitute or a homosexual male. This was the teaching of Baal which was, apparently, brought right into the house of God.

Did Nothing About It. Eli knew what his sons were doing and didn't do anything about it. Eli had no firm hand upon his out-of-control sons who *"brought their mother to shame."* The father, who was a priest of God, said too little and too late. It is like the man who gave us our syrup this morning for our french toast. When the squeezer was leaking all over the table he finally brought us a tomato catsup bottle. I said *"We don't want any tomato catsup."* He told us there was good syrup in it. The remark he made was too little and too late because we had finished our breakfast.

Too Late. And so it was with Eli's sons. Eli's sons did not harken to their father because, at this time in their lives, it was too late. Eli did not *"chasten his sons betimes,"* or early enough. It was not done early in their lives, so they were out-of-hand at this time in their lives. God spoke to Eli. He reproved him and asked him why he honored his sons above Him. In effect, the Lord wondered why Eli was afraid of his sons, but was not afraid of the Lord. Eli's sons took the best cuts of the meat of the sacrifices before it was boiled. This was supposed to be given to the Lord. That's why later on it says that Eli was an *"old man and heavy"* because probably he ate too much of the meat of the offerings of the Lord. He fell over backwards and broke his neck.

"And it came to pass, when he made mention of the ark of God, that he fell from off the seat backward by the side of the gate, and **his neck brake**, and he died: for **he was an old man, and heavy**. And he had judged Israel forty years." (1 Samuel 4:18)

God's Judgment. God fulfilled the judgment upon Eli's two sons. The slaying of Eli's sons is a bad example of how **not** to make a marriage "melodious" by multiplying it to our children. How could a marriage of these two sons be "melodious" when they were filled with sin. No matter what Eli's own marriage might have been, there was certainly no "melodious multiplication" to his sons in this case. It is quite likely, judging from the product in his sons, that Eli and his wife had failed the Lord greatly.

Chapter Four—Multiplication of a Melodious Marriage

b. The Sinning--Samuel's Sons.

(1 Samuel 8:1-5) (8:1) *"And it came to pass, when Samuel was old, that he made his sons judges over Israel . . . . (8:3) And his sons walked not in his ways, but turned aside after lucre, and took bribes, and perverted judgment. (8:5a) And said* [that is, the elders of Israel,] *unto him, Behold, thou art old, and thy sons walk not in thy ways: . ."*

Eli Had A Second Chance. In a real sense, Eli had a second chance when raising Samuel there in the temple. But Eli's example of how to be a father to his own sons was a bad example. It did not teach Samuel how to be a good father. It takes two to raise a proper son--a good father and a good mother. Where was Mrs. Eli when her sons misbehaved in the tabernacle and in other places? Where was Mrs. Samuel when Samuel was off in his "ministry" and she was left alone to take care of her children?

Samuel Was All Right. Samuel was a good judge. He was a good little boy when he was young. The Lord spoke to him and called to him four times, if you remember. For the first three times, Samuel thought Eli called him, so he went to Eli when he heard his name. Eli said I didn't call you. He went back and forth three different times. Finally Eli got the message that it was the Lord who was talking to Samuel. Little Samuel was open to the things of God when he was young. When he was old, he made his sons judges over Israel in his place. His sons took bribes which perverted their judgment.

Not Walking in Our Ways. What a terrible thing for us to hear, as parents, that our sons or our daughters *"walk not in our ways."* Of course maybe they do walk in our ways and our ways are not right! That's another angle, isn't it. May your ways and my ways always please the Lord so that our children might walk in the ways that their parents have set forth. *"Train up a child in the way he should go and when he is old he will not depart from it"* (Proverbs 22:6). Samuel did not do what God told him to do in the chastening of his sons. His sons got away from him. It was too late, then. I hope it is not too late for your children or your grandchildren so that you can pray for them and influence them to follow the Lord Jesus Christ and His will and ways.

● **2. GOOD EXAMPLES OF BRINGING UP CHILDREN:**

a. The Serving--Ruth.

(Ruth 1:16-17) (1:16) *"And Ruth said, Intreat me not to leave thee, or to return from following after thee, for whither thou goest, I will go; and where thou lodgest, I will lodge: thy people shall be my people, and THY GOD MY*

GOD: (1:17) *Where thou diest, will I die, and there will I be buried: the Lord do so to me, and more also, if ought but death part thee and me."*

Ruth Had a Heritage. Ruth was not a child. She was a heathen Moabitess. But she may have been an obedient child as she was growing up as evidenced by what she said and what she did when with Naomi. Sometimes Ruth 1:16 is used in weddings. Ruth was talking to her mother-in-law, Naomi, who had lost her husband and her sons. Ruth had also lost her husband. Naomi said that Ruth and Orpah should leave her because their husbands were dead. She said she had no more sons and even if she were to have another son, they would be too old for him when he grew up. She told them to go back home to their heathen gods.

Naomi's Bitterness. What a testimony Naomi must have had, even though she was bitter. She said, *"Call me not Naomi* ['pleasant'] *call me Mara* ['bitter']" (Ruth 1:20). That's what she said when she went home to Bethlehem. She possessed qualities within her, even in her bitterness, that made Ruth, a heathen unsaved woman, take notice that she had a true God and a true faith. Ruth wanted to follow her. I wonder if our children (or our children-in-law) would find such admirable qualities in us? Ruth said: *"whither thou goest, I will go."* She also said: *"thy people shall be my people, and THY GOD MY GOD."* This is a tremendous testimony that Ruth had. Ruth wanted to serve the Lord because she saw some good qualities in Naomi which Naomi had passed on to Ruth.

---

b.   The Searching--Joshua & Caleb.

(Numbers 14:6-9) (14:6) *"And Joshua the son of Nun, and Caleb the son of Jephunneh, which were of them that **searched** the land, rent their clothes. (14:7) And they spake unto all the company of the children of Israel, saying, The land, which we passed through to search it, is an exceeding good land. (14:8) If the LORD delight in us, then he will bring us into this land, and give it us; a land which floweth with milk and honey. (14:9) Only rebel not ye against the LORD, neither fear ye the people of the land; for they are bread for us: their defence is departed from them, and the LORD is with us: fear them not."*

Joshua and Caleb. Joshua and Caleb were not children. They were men, probably in their forties. Many years earlier, they had a childhood. They were products of that childhood. In them, there was a multiplication of what must have been a "melodious marriage" of their parents. The context, as you know, was at Kadeshbarnea (Numbers 13:26; 32:8). God wanted the children of Israel to go into the land of Canaan. This was the Land of Promise. It was a land flowing *"with milk and honey."*

Chapter Four—Multiplication of a Melodious Marriage

Ten out of Twelve. Twelve spies were sent out to search out the land. Ten of the spies came back with a negative report concerning the land and the battle that would have to be waged in order to capture it. Two of the twelve, however, came back (named Joshua and Caleb) who brought a positive report of the land and the success the Lord would give them in the battle for it. We would assume that Joshua and Caleb had a proper upbringing in the things of the Lord. They could see the power of God, the blessings of God, and the victory of God over all the enemies that were in the land of Canaan. The ten could not see this, perhaps, because they had an upbringing that was wrong and false. There was no "melodious marriage" in their homes. They did not have good and godly homes as children.

Grapes or Giants? All the ten spies could see were the giants who were in the land. But Joshua and Caleb focused upon the good grapes and the good fruit they had found in Canaan. They said that the Lord would give the Israelites this land. They had some vision and insight. May the Lord give us some vision and insight. Joshua and Caleb were no doubt brought up right in the things of the Lord. We ought to have more Joshua's and Caleb's today! There were only these two out of that whole generation that entered into the Land of Promise. Joshua was the leader who led the children of Israel into Canaan. Caleb went with him also. At the age of 80, Caleb wanted to take the mountain at Hebron for his possession, though there were many enemies there. He said *"Give me this mountain"* (Joshua 14:12). He fought at the age of 80 for a mountain site in the land of promise and was victorious. He was a great and faithful man.

---

c. The Steadfastness--Daniel.

(Daniel 1:8; 6:10) (1:8) *"But Daniel purposed in his heart that he would not defile himself with the portion of the king's meat, nor with the wine which he drank; therefore he requested of the prince of the eunuchs that he might not defile himself. . . .* (6:10) *Now when Daniel knew that the writing was signed, he went into his house; and his windows being open in his chamber toward Jerusalem, he kneeled upon his knees three times a day, and prayed, and gave thanks before his God, as he did aforetime."*

Daniel Was Trained Well. He had a proper upbringing. Daniel was not a child. He was a man. It has been rightly said that men are just *"big children."* Every man or woman has a childhood. Everyone used to be a child who had an upbringing. Sometimes people have had a bad upbringing. They have had to break out of that upbringing in order to serve the Lord. Maybe this is true of you.

Daniel Stood for the Lord. Daniel was one of the captives who was brought to Babylon during the 70 years that Israel was in captivity to the kingdom of Babylon. Daniel was a wise man. He knew learning. All of those who were brought to the king's palace had great wisdom and understanding. Notice Daniel was told he had to eat *"a portion of the king's meat."* This might have been pork, or some other meat which was unclean. He steadfastly refused such meat. He requested "pulse" or vegetables to eat instead of meat (Daniel 1:12). You can live on vegetable protein. You don't have to have animal protein in order to live and stay healthy. Cows do this all the time. *"Daniel purposed in his heart that he would not defile himself."*

The Jealous Princes. You know the story. There was jealousy among the princes of Babylon. They had to find out something against this young man. He was brought up in such a great way that they couldn't find anything against him except in the law of his God. What a testimony! I wonder if that same principle were applied to us, what would happen? These princes had the king make a decree that nobody could ask anything of any God or any person except the king. That sounded good to that puffed-up king. He was very proud, arrogant, and haughty until the Lord humbled him and brought him low.

The Habit of Prayer. These princes knew this would get to Daniel. They knew that Daniel was faithful to the Lord, and therefore would violate the decree of the king. Daniel went to his room, even though he knew he was not supposed to ask anything of anyone except the king, and he prayed to the Lord. His windows were opened facing Jerusalem. This is the place where he prayed three times a day. These men knew Daniel would do this. They waited and watched him pray and then reported him to the king for punishment. Do people know that you and I are going to be faithful to our God? I hope so.

Removing the Coat. Do you know the story about the three forces that were trying to get the coat off a man? The wind blew, but the man wrapped the coat around him even tighter. The rain came, but again, the man wrapped his coat around him more firmly. Finally, the sun succeeded in getting the man to remove his coat. It shined warmly on the man. With this, the man voluntarily removed his coat. Sometimes, when someone tells us to do something we are stronger then ever before in doing the opposite.

Resistance Brings Strength. For instance, if someone tells us not to pray, that should make us stronger in our faith. It should. We should do it even more determinedly because it is right. Daniel with great reverence and desire continued as he did aforetime. I hope that this is your style. I hope that when people say you shouldn't witness, shouldn't read your Bible, shouldn't go to church, shouldn't honor your mother and your father, shouldn't have a faithful home before the Lord, or shouldn't Scripturally discipline your children, that you are strong and even more determined to do what is right. If you are doing what is wrong and someone admonishes you, I hope that you change your

Chapter Four—Multiplication of a Melodious Marriage

actions and do what is right. If you are doing what is right and some people don't like it, that's too bad. If God likes it and it is in the Word of God, then we must stand and be steadfast like Daniel.

d. The Standing--Shadrach, Meshach, & Abednego.

(Daniel 3:16-18) (3:16) *"Shadrach, Meshach, and Abednego, answered and said to the king, O Nebuchadnezzar, we are not careful to answer thee in this matter.* (3:17) *If it be so, our God whom we serve is able to deliver us from the burning fiery furnace, and we will deliver us out of thine hand, O king.* (3:18) *But if not, be it known unto thee, O king, that we will not serve thy gods, nor worship the golden image which thou hast set up."*

Refusing Evil. You know this story also. These three Hebrew young men were told to bow down to the image of Nebuchadnezzar. They refused to do so because they were Hebrews. God had said to them in His Word concerning images and idols:

"Thou shalt not bow down thyself to them, nor serve them: for I the LORD thy God *am* a jealous God . . ."(Exodus 20:5).

Burned Alive. Daniel was sent to the den of lions for violating the king's command. Regardless of the consequences, Daniel went ahead and did what God wanted him to do. He let the Lord take care of any consequences that might result in his doing that which was right. Daniel escaped from the den of lions victoriously because God protected him. For not bowing down to the large image, Shadrach, Meshach, and Abednego faced being burned alive in a fiery furnace.

To Bow or Not To Bow. The three men told the king that they were not going to bow down and worship the king's image, no matter what he might do to them. They took a proper stand and position on this. They were young men who were, evidently, brought up properly. They had a good upbringing as children. They followed the Lord. God spared their lives, too. They told the king that even if God didn't spare their lives, they would not bow down or worship the king's image. We may have to face such persecution here in our United States of America if things continue as they are. We must be prepared to stand for the Lord and His Words.

C. OTHER THOUGHTS FOR HELPING OUR CHILDREN:

● 1. <u>Support</u>. Children from church homes need our support. All the world is against them--the children at school, their playmates, maybe even other adults. Support them.

● 2. <u>Surrender</u>. By all means, instill in your children that they must first be saved, and then surrender their spirits, their souls, and their bodies to the Lord Jesus Christ. God is not pleased with anything else but total surrender.

● 3. <u>Success</u>. Wish for success for your children. Not the material success that the world seeks, but success with the Lord, as Joshua 1:8 talks about. *"Then thou shalt make thy way prosperous, and then thou shalt have good success."*

● 4. <u>Study</u>. Encourage your children to study the Word of God. *"Study to shew thyself approved unto God, a workman that needeth not to be ashamed, rightly dividing the Word of truth."*

● 5. <u>Stubbornness</u>. You must seek to eliminate this trait if used in the wrong way. We must be steadfast and strong for the Lord, but not stubborn.

● 6. <u>Safety</u>. Keep your children safe and in safe surroundings. Guard them carefully. Don't let them wander the streets at all hours of the day or night like some other mothers and fathers do. Keep them safe from harm in your home. Protect them.

● 7. <u>Schedule</u>. Seek to inculcate into your children's hearts the idea of a schedule. This includes such things as prayer time, studying the Word of God, playing, doing their homework, and doing their chores around the house. A schedule is important to children.

● 8. <u>Sample</u>. May your children be good samples of what good Christian young people ought to be. Encourage them in that way.

● 9. <u>Schooling</u>. Be concerned about your children's schooling. Be concerned about their Bible schooling as well. Be interested in where they go to school. If they go to a Christian college urge them to pick a college that glorifies the Lord Jesus Christ. Preferably, it should be an institution that uses and defends the King James Bible and teaches the same strong Biblical standards that you have in your home.

● 10. <u>Sanctuary</u>. Take your children to go to the sanctuary of their God (a Bible-believing and preaching local church) on a regular basis with you. When they leave your home, hopefully, they will continue to do this.

● 11. <u>Scrapping</u>. When your children scrap and fight (and they will scrap and fight if you have several of them), seek what you can do to avoid that and to calm them down. The Lord must give you plenty of wisdom and determination for this.

Chapter Four—Multiplication of a Melodious Marriage 77

● **12.** <u>Satisfaction</u>. Be satisfied with your children. Find in them the greatest satisfaction. This should be especially true for you mothers. My wife wanted to be whatever the Lord had for her. She yielded her life to serve the Lord when and where He chose. Now she is the mother of our five children and married to a preacher. She realized that "mothering" was a ministry as well as a mission field. Be satisfied with your children. Be satisfied with what the Lord has given you. Mothering is an important ministry.

● **13.** <u>Security</u>. Give your children the security that you love them and care for them. Be concerned for their welfare, and for their well-being.

● **14.** <u>Self- confidence</u>. Your children need self-confidence. Many people might run them down. They might tell them they look bad, they smell bad, they think bad. Give them self-confidence. You can discipline them and spank them as needed in the proper manner, but also give them some self-confidence.

● **15.** <u>Self-control</u>. Your children need self-control, just like we adults need self-control. Try to build it into their lives so that they can control themselves. In so doing, they will not need to be disciplined.

● **16.** <u>Self-esteem</u>. This is not in a bad sense like Robert Schuler's modernism. Your children should have a certain self-esteem, even though they have a sin nature, so that they feel valuable to themselves, to others, and to the Lord. This is important.

● **17.** <u>Self-respect</u>. Your children must respect their worth as individuals and as Christians, if they are saved. They should not drag the Name of the Lord Jesus Christ into the dust by their actions or inactions.

● **18.** <u>Self-sufficiency</u>. Build within your children, not a complete dependency upon you, but a self-sufficiency so that they may make their own decisions, based on the Word of God.

● **19.** <u>Scripture</u>. Instill within the hearts of your children a love for Scripture and reading the Word of God.

● **20.** <u>Sermons</u>. Take your children to where they can listen to good and godly sermons from a pastor who preaches and teaches the Word of God from the King James Bible, preferably in a verse-by-verse manner through Bible books. Let them not criticize and disdain sermons and preaching of the Word.

● **21.** <u>Spirituality</u>. May it be a desire on your part that your children have a spirituality about them because they are led by the Spirit of God, and are filled by the Spirit of God. May they want to please the Lord Jesus Christ in all things.

● **22.** <u>Shamefulness</u>. There is lots of shamefulness all around this world where your children go. Try to keep them from it. If need be, warn them concerning some of this shamefulness that they will hear and see. Pull them away from it, and protect them from this shamefulness wherever possible.

● 23.   **Shelter.** Make sure your home is always a shelter and a place of protection for your children. No matter where they go, they might get the stones and arrows of outrageous fortune, as some have written, but in the home, there must be a shelter for them.

● 24.   **Shyness.** Some of our children are shyer then others. Yet there are some whom you wish would be a little more shy. Try to overcome any shyness, so that they would be bold for the Lord, and be good witnesses for Christ.

● 25.   **Stability.** Give your children stability by your stability. Stability breeds stability, just like confidence breeds confidence, and love breeds love. Encourage them.

● 26.   **Stigma.** Because they are Fundamentalist children from Fundamentalist parents who are separated and love the Lord, they are going to have a stigma about them, even from Christian people, if they stand upon the Word of God. Some of the Christians might say that they are too straight-laced. You must build them up. Tell them that is all right to stand where God wants us to stand, no matter what the price. Give them that encouragement.

● 27.   **Sorrow.** Your children might have much sorrow. Some young people seem to be made of sorrow and disappointment. You comfort them as a parent, and understand when they are sorrowful.

● 28.   **Strategy.** Have a strategy that will encourage your children to be the best that they can be for the Lord. You should plan and have a strategy toward this goal.

Conclusion

Our Theme. Our theme has been making our marriage melodious. You can make a marriage all right. We want a "melodious marriage." When in captivity, Israel did not want to sing the Lord's song because they were in a "strange land."

> *"We hanged our harps upon the willows in the midst thereof. For there they that carried us away captive required of us a song; and they that wasted us required of us mirth, saying, Sing us one of the songs of Zion. How shall we sing the LORD'S song in a strange land?"* (Psalm 137:2-4)

Chapter Four–Multiplication of a Melodious Marriage

Keep Harping! Never hang up your "harps" in your marriage! Keep the melody ringing in your hearts and in your homes. Here are some beautiful words from one of our gospel songs that we sing often:

"I have a song that Jesus gave me. It was sent from Heaven above. There never was a sweeter melody. 'Tis a melody of love. In my heart there rings a melody. There rings a melody of Heaven's harmony. In my heart there rings a melody. There rings a melody of love."

If you are saved, you can say these words, and you can sing them as well. By God's grace and with God's help, keep up your daily practice of "MAKING MARRIAGE MELODIOUS"! You can do it if you determine to keep trying day by day with God's help!

Index of Words and Phrases

1 Corinthians 7	9, 12, 39, 41, 42, 46, 48, 53
12 months	51
1611	12
1918-1958	37
1948	3, 55
1949	33, 59
1951	59
1954	59
1956	3, 60
1965	59
1978	15
1985	56
1987	ix
20's	28
3,000	3, 23, 45
3,000 and 4,000	45
3,000 to 4,000	3, 23
4,000	3, 23, 45
40's	28
40%	40
40th class reunion	37
50's	44
54 years	2
68 Hints for Women	24
80	vii, 73
Abednego	vii, 75
Abraham	22
active duty	3, 23, 31, 34, 45, 46, 51
Adam	7, 9-17, 21, 40, 41
admonition	64, 67, 68
adulterers	39, 40, 42
adulterous affair	34
adultery	3, 4, 28, 30, 34-36, 52, 70
affair	34
age of 80	73
AKRASIAN	51, 52
always	3, 12, 20, 24, 29, 32, 33, 45, 51, 55, 60, 61, 63, 65, 67, 68, 70, 71, 78
androgyny	6
angry	20, 53

Making Marriage Melodious

animate	8
Arabian Proverb	37
arrangement	27
Assistant Pastor	60
Assistant to the Director	60
Atlantic ocean	31
attitude	26, 61, 63
authority	24, 45, 46, 53, 61
avoiding fornication	41
Baal	69, 70
Bakker, James	52
Baptist	viii, ix, 8, 23, 24, 34, 35, 60
Baptist church	viii, ix, 8, 24, 34, 60
Beethoven	2
Belial	69
benevolence	43-46
bestiality	9, 10
betimes	63, 65, 66, 70
BFT	1, iii, ix, 15, 23, 24, 38
BFT #3006	1, iii
BFT #623	24, 38
BFT #697	23
Bible classes	24, 31
Bible For Today	iii, viii, ix, 15, 60, 66
Bible For Today Baptist Church	viii, ix, 60
Bible For Today Press	iii
Billy James Hargis	23
bishop	24, 33-36
bitter	53, 72
blame	13, 14, 17, 52
blasphemy	40
board of education	65
bodily resurrection	60
body	6, 8, 15, 17, 25, 27-29, 33, 36, 43, 45, 46, 53, 56
Boston	34
boundaries	9, 44
bow down	75
Bremerhaven, Germany	31
Bridgeport, Connecticut	15
bring them up	62
cacophony	2, 64
Caleb	vii, 72, 73

Index of Words and Phrases

```
camp ........................................... ix, 55
Canaan ......................................... 72, 73
cancer ............................................. 56
cantankerous ....................................... 53
castaway ........................................... 36
chasten ............................................ 66
chasteneth ................................. 63, 65, 66
chemotherapy ....................................... 56
cherish ........................................ 29, 62
child discipline .................................... 64
child training ..................................... 64
children ............ vii, 1, 3, 7, 13, 21, 22, 25, 29, 31, 33, 34, 38, 59-78
Christian husband ............... 19, 20, 25, 27, 29, 30, 37, 42, 43, 45
Christian mates .................................... 47
Christian wife ................. 19, 20, 25, 27-29, 34, 37, 43
Christian women ....................... 19, 20, 30, 33
clarinet ............................................. 2
cleave ............................................. 11
coats of skins ................................. 15-17
cohabit ............................................ 51
Collingswood, NJ .................................... ix
come together again ......................... 47, 49-51
Composer ............................................ 1
compromise .................................... 21, 34
Conclusion .................................... 20, 78
consent ................................... 47, 49, 50
continuous ............................ 42-49, 51, 62
continuous action ................. 42, 43, 45-49, 51, 62
corporal punishment ..................... 61, 63, 67
correcteth ......................................... 63
correction .................................. 64, 66-68
Council of Eighteen, of GARBC ...................... 35
counsel ............................................ 64
counseling sessions ................................ 23
cows ............................................... 74
created .............................. 5, 6, 9, 14, 41
creation ..................................... 5, 7, 8
cremation .......................................... 15
*Cremation, Is It Christian?* ....................... 15
crematory .......................................... 15
Crosby, Fanny ...................................... 15
cultural .................................. 19, 20, 24
```

Dallas Theological Seminary 33, 34, 53
Dan 59, 60
Daniel .... vii, viii, 73-75
daughter .... ix, 3, 59, 60, 65
Dave 59, 60
deacon 15, 34
debt 44, 45
deep sleep 10, 17
defraud 47, 50
DeHaan, Dr. M. R. 16
Deity of Christ 60
delight 59, 64, 68, 72
den of lions 75
Detroit Bible Class 16
Devil 14, 21, 23, 68
Dianne .... viii, 60
Dick 59, 60
discipline 61, 63-68, 74, 77
disciplining 63
Divine image 6
divorce 11, 12, 30, 31, 53
dominion 45, 46, 53
Don 59, 60
Dr. DeHaan 16
Dr. Erwin Moon 8
Dr. Harold John Ockenga 8
Dr. M. R. DeHaan 16
Dr. Ockenga 8
duet 1, 27, 64
duties .... vi, vii, 19, 26, 31, 60, 61, 63
duty 3, 19, 22, 23, 31, 34, 44-46, 51, 66
Eden 8-10, 16, 21, 40
eight verses 64
EKTREPHETE 62
Eli 69-71
England 31
Ephesians 19-22, 25, 27, 54, 60, 62-64
evangelist 46
evangelist in uniform 46
Eve 7, 9, 10, 12-14, 16, 17, 21, 40, 41
evolution 7, 8
evolved 5, 8

Index of Words and Phrases

Faith Baptist Church	8
faithful	2, 42, 54, 56, 60, 68, 73, 74
false teaching	20, 21, 40
Fanny Crosby	15
fasting and prayer	47, 49
fathers	x, 11, 13, 60, 61, 76
fear	20, 26, 31, 72
fiery furnace	75
fig leaves	13
first marriage	10, 41
first person	ix
flat	2
Florida	23, 51, 60
foolishness	4, 66
for a time	47, 49, 50
force	48, 61-63
forgiveness	54
fornication	3, 28, 39, 41, 70
fornicators	42
foundations of marriage	5
Four Rules When Disciplining	63
fruit trees	9
Fundamentalist	34, 78
GARBC	23, 35
garden	8-10, 12, 16, 17, 21, 40
garden of Eden	8-10, 16, 21, 40
gave	viii-10, 12, 13, 15, 21, 23, 24, 27, 29, 33, 42, 45, 66, 68, 70, 73, 79
gay	6, 23
gay rights	6, 23
Gay Rights Movement	6
Germany	31
Ghandi	15
giants	73
glue	30, 31
Gospel of Luke	53
Gospel of Mark	53
grandchildren	3, 59, 60, 71
grapes	73
Greek	6, 12, 22, 23, 25, 26, 29, 39, 40, 42-49, 51, 57, 60, 62-64
Hargis, Billy James	23
harmonize	49
harmony	2, 3, 27, 33, 64, 79

harps	78
head	25-28, 33, 63
headship	25-27
heavy	70
Hebrew	8, 12, 26, 42, 57, 65, 67, 75
Helen Waite	37
hell	64, 67
Hindus	15
Hodgkin's disease	56
homosexual sin	40
homosexuality	6, 9, 10, 40, 41
honor	32, 33, 51, 74
honour	32, 33, 53
honourable in all	39, 40
HUPOTASSESTHAI	25
HUPOTASSO	24
husband	1, 2, 7, 11, 12, 14, 17, 19-21, 24-30, 33, 34, 37, 39, 41-46, 48, 50-55, 72
Husband-Loving Lessons	55
hymn	2
hypocrisy	35
Illinois	3
In My Heart There Rings a Melody	79
inanimate	8
incontinency	47, 49, 51
inerrant	42, 60
inerrant Word of God	60
Introductory Comments	v, 1
Jeanette	59
Jim Bakker	52
Joshua	vii, 72, 73, 76
jurisdiction	45, 53
King James Bible	12, 42, 76, 77
knowledge of good and evil	9, 21
Kristen	60
lack of control	54
laetrile	56
laryngitis	2
leave	11, 29, 30, 35, 62, 71, 72, 76
lesbian	6, 7, 23, 25
lesbian Virginia Mollenkott	23, 25
lesbianism	10

Index of Words and Phrases

liberation	19, 32
life boat	31
Lorraine	59
lost chord	2
love	7, 11, 14, 26-30, 40-55, 65-67, 77-79
love relationship	48, 54
lymph glands	56
maker	v, 4, 5, 7, 17, 19, 37, 59
Making Marriage Melodious	ix
managers	vi, 4, 19, 20, 26, 37, 55, 59
manual	v, 4
map	v, 4
Mara	72
marine	23, 51
Marine Corps	23
Marine Corps Air Station	23
marines	46, 51
marriage	1, iii, v-vii, ix, x, 1-5, 7, 10-12, 19, 20, 24, 26-32, 37-46, 48, 51-56, 59, 60, 64, 69, 70, 78, 79
marriage disaster	53
marriage vows	20, 54, 56
married love	40-54
mate	9, 10, 30, 45, 47-49, 52-54, 56, 57
maturity	29, 30, 62, 63
Megan	60
melody	2, 3, 33, 56, 79
men-haters	22
Meshach	vii, 75
Miami, Florida	51
Military Sea Transportation Service	31
misanthropic	23
Mollenkott, Virginia	6, 23, 25
monkey	10
Moody Bible Institute	8
Moon, Dr. Irwin	8
mountain	38, 73
mountains	38
Mrs. Ghandi	15
Mrs. Waite	3, 15, 23, 33, 34
multiplication	vii, 4, 59, 60, 68, 69, 72
music	v, 1-3
music and marriage	v

mutuality .... vi, 4, 14, 37, 38, 45, 54, 55, 59
my mother 37
my wife .... viii, 15, 23, 24, 26, 31, 33, 34, 38, 44-46, 48, 51, 55, 56, 77
naked 13, 17
Naomi 72
Naval Chaplain 3, 31, 34, 45, 46, 51
navy 23, 46, 51
Nebuchadnezzar 75
negative 47, 48, 51, 60, 73
neo-evangelical 34
Neo-Evangelicalism 8
New Jersey .... iii, 23
Newton 8
Newton, Massachusetts 8
next generation 60
nourish 62
NOUTHESIA 64
nurture 63, 68
obedience 20, 22, 25, 65
obey 20, 22
obeyed 20, 22
Ockenga, Dr. Harold John 8, 34
off-key 2, 64
Ohio ix
Okinawa 31, 51
one flesh 11, 12, 17, 29, 32
only .. 2, 3, 5, 9, 12, 16, 19, 22, 24-26, 30, 31, 34, 35, 40, 42, 45, 47, 49, 50,
                                54-57, 62, 63, 65, 67, 69, 72, 73
Opalocka 23
orchestra 1
Orpah 72
PAIDEIA 63
parents 11, 17, 21, 22, 29, 60, 61, 66, 68, 71, 72, 78
Park Street Church 8, 34
pastor .... 1, iii, viii, ix, 8, 23, 24, 28, 34-36, 60, 69, 77
Pastor D. A. Waite .... 1, iii, ix
Patterson State College 23
PEIRAZO 51
Pennsylvania 62
permitted areas of force 62
Ph.D. .... 1, iii, ix, 23, 57
Ph.D. in speech 57

Index of Words and Phrases

Philadelphia 61, 65-67
PHOBETAI 26
practice 1-3, 9, 11, 15, 29, 38, 47, 79
prayer 47, 49-51, 53, 74, 76
preachers 20, 24, 25
present tense 22, 42, 43, 45-49, 51, 60-62
prohibition 47, 48, 60, 61
prostitution 70
Proverbs .... x, 63-68, 71
Proverbs 18:22 x
Proverbs 19:14 x
Proverbs 5:18 x
qualifications .... v, 3
quartet 1, 64
quintet 1, 64
Radio Bible Class 16
record-holders 32, 33
Reggie 60
remain single 53
render 43-46
reproof 64, 67
resurrection 60
reverence 26, 74
re-marry 53
rhythm 3
rib 10, 41
right ... 3, 9, 12, 20, 21, 25-28, 32, 33, 35, 36, 39, 46, 50, 55, 56, 59, 61-63,
                                                   65, 66, 70, 71, 73-75, 78
Ringwood, New Jersey 6
rod 63-67
Roman Catholic Church 40, 41
Romans 7 53
rule 14, 21, 34, 35, 45, 46, 53, 61
Ruth .... vii, 71, 72
sacrifice .... vi, 15-17, 27, 69
Samuel 69-71
sanctification .... vi, 28
sanctify 28
Sarah 22, 23
Satan 12, 17, 47, 49, 51-54
saved 30, 31, 41, 76, 77, 79
scales 2, 3

seat of learning	65
second adultery	35
selfish	28
selfishness	vi, 28, 29
serpent	12-14, 17
sex	38, 70
sex education	38
sextet	1, 64
sexual love	40, 44
sexual needs	39
sexual relations	39-41, 44
sexuality	vi, 32, 39
Shadrach	vii, 75
shame	v, vii, 12, 13, 17, 25, 64, 67, 68, 70
sharp	2
shelter	29, 62, 78
Shelton College	6
shifting	v, 13, 14, 17
shifting blame	14
shut up	44, 45
silent	25, 55
single	9, 33, 45, 53
sleep	10, 17
sodomy	9, 10
solo	1, 2, 27, 64
songs of Zion	78
soul	v, 6, 8, 17, 64, 66-69
sound track	3
spanking	vii, 61, 63
sparing	vii, 65, 68
speaking	vii, 3, 22, 28, 48, 50, 64, 65, 67
spies	73
spoiling	vii, 66, 68
spot	28
stick	3, 11, 30, 31
stop defrauding	48
storm	31
submission	vi, 14, 19-22, 38
submit	17, 19-22
subordination	vi, 25
sub-man	8
sub-man theory	8

Index of Words and Phrases

summary	v, vi, 5, 17, 46
Sunday School	25
SUNERCHO	51
synthesis	v, 7
Table of Contents	v
Tammy	52
teach	6, 8, 11, 19, 20, 24, 25, 37, 46, 53, 60, 66-68, 71
teach classes	24
temple prostitution	70
test	51
the score	1
theistic evolution	8
thou	9, 13, 16, 60, 64, 67, 71, 72, 75, 76
three mountains of marriage	38
time	3-7, 15, 22, 24, 28, 30, 31, 34-36, 42, 45, 47, 49-52, 55-57, 60, 61, 65, 66, 69, 70, 74, 76
topsy	65
trio	1, 64
tripartite	6
U. S. Marines	51
unequally yoked	48
unisex	6
University of Michigan	16
usurp	24
usurp authority	24
vegetable protein	74
vegetables	74
verses on marriage	x
Virginia Mollenkott	6, 23, 25
vows	11, 20, 31, 54, 56
walks on the right	33
wall	48, 53
weaker vessel	17, 32, 53
what	4, 8-11, 13, 15, 16, 19, 20, 23, 25-30, 32, 34, 38, 39, 41-49, 51-54, 57, 59-61, 63, 65-72, 74-78
when	ix, 1-3, 7, 8, 12, 15, 17, 20, 21, 23-25, 27-31, 33-36, 39-46, 50, 52, 55, 56, 61-74, 76-78
wife	viii, x, 1, 2, 11, 13-15, 17, 19-21, 23-35, 37-39, 41-46, 48, 50-56, 70, 77
wives	vi, 19-23, 26-30, 32-34, 38, 41, 44, 45, 48, 51, 53, 54, 56, 59
woman	4, 6, 10-14, 17, 20, 21, 23, 24, 29-32, 35, 39, 41, 42, 44, 48, 72, 73
women liberationists	6

women preachers 24, 25
Women, Men, and the Bible 6, 25
women's liberation 32
World Almanac 32
wrinkle 28
wrong beat 2
ye 12, 22, 32, 39, 42, 47-49, 53, 54, 60, 69, 72
Zion 78
"mutual submission" 20, 21

About the Author

The author of this book, Dr. D. A. Waite, received a B.A. (Bachelor of Arts) in classical Greek and Latin from the University of Michigan in 1948, a Th.M. (Master of Theology), with high honors, in New Testament Greek Literature and Exegesis from Dallas Theological Seminary in 1952, an M.A. (Master of Arts) in Speech from Southern Methodist University in 1953, a Th.D. (Doctor of Theology), with honors, in Bible Exposition from Dallas Theological Seminary in 1955, and a Ph.D. in Speech from Purdue University in 1961. He holds both New Jersey and Pennsylvania teacher certificates in Greek and Language Arts.

He has been a teacher in the areas of Greek, Hebrew, Bible, Speech, and English for over fifty-two years in ten schools, including one junior high, one senior high, three Bible institutes, two colleges, two universities, and one seminary. He served his country as a Navy Chaplain for five years on active duty; pastored three churches; was Chairman and Director of the Radio and Audio-Film Commission of the American Council of Christian Churches; since 1971, has been Founder, President, and Director of THE BIBLE FOR TODAY; since 1978, has been President of the DEAN BURGON SOCIETY; has produced over 700 other studies, books, cassettes, or VCR's on various topics; and is heard on both a five-minute daily and thirty-minute weekly radio program IN DEFENSE OF TRADITIONAL BIBLE TEXTS, presently on 25 stations. Dr. and Mrs. Waite have been married since 1948; they have four sons, one daughter, and, at present, eight grandchildren. Since October 4, 1998, he founded and has been the Pastor of the Bible For Today Baptist Church in Collingswood, New Jersey. His sermons are heard both on radio and the Internet over "www.BibleForToday.org/audio_sermons.htm"

Order Blank (p. 1)

Name:_____

Address:_____

City & State:_____ Zip:_____

*Credit Card #:*_____*Expires:*_____

Materials You Should Order

[ ] Send *Making Marriage Melodious* by Pastor D. A. Waite ($7+$3 S&H), perfect bound, 112 pages.
[ ] Send *Ephesians--Preaching Verse by Verse* by Pastor D. A. Waite ($12+$5 S&H) hardback, 224 pages.
[ ] Send *Galatians--Preaching Verse By Verse* by Pastor D. A. Waite ($12+$5 S&H) hardback, 216 pages.
[ ] Send *First Peter--Preaching Verse By Verse* by Pastor D. A. Waite ($10+$5 S&H) hardback, 176 pages.
[ ] Send *Fundamentalist MIS-INFORMATION on Bible Versions* by Dr. Waite ($7+$3 S&H) perfect bound, 136 pages
[ ] Send *Holes in the Holman Christian Standard Bible* by Dr. Waite ($3+$2 S&H) A printed booklet, 40 pages
[ ] Send *Central Seminary Refuted on Bible Versions* by Dr. Waite ($10+$3 S&H) A perfect bound book, 184 pages
[ ] Send *Fundamentalist Distortions on Bible Versions* by Dr. Waite ($6+$3 S&H) A perfect bound book, 80 pages
[ ] Send *Burgon's Warnings on Revision* by DAW ($7+$3 S&H) A perfect bound book, 120 pages in length.
[ ] Send *The Case for the King James Bible* by DAW ($7+$3 S&H) A perfect bound book, 112 pages in length.
[ ] Send *Foes of the King James Bible Refuted* by DAW ($10+$4 S&H) A perfect bound book, 164 pages in length.
[ ] Send *The Revision Revised* by Dean Burgon ($25 + $4 S&H) A hardback book, 640 pages in length.
[ ] Send *The Last 12 Verses of Mark* by Dean Burgon ($15+$4 S&H) A hardback book 400 pages.

Send or Call Orders to:
THE BIBLE FOR TODAY
900 Park Ave., Collingswood, NJ 08108
Phone: 856-854-4452; FAX:--2464; Orders: 1-800 JOHN 10:9
E-Mail Orders: BFT@BibleForToday.org; Credit Cards O K

Order Blank (p. 2)

Name:_____

Address:_____

City & State:_____Zip:_____

Credit Card #:_____Expires:_____

Other Materials on the KJB & T.R.

[ ] Send *The Traditional Text* hardback by Burgon ($16 + $4 S&H) A hardback book, 384 pages in length.
[ ] Send *Causes of Corruption* by Burgon ($15 + $4 S&H) A hardback book, 360 pages in length.
[ ] Send *Inspiration and Interpretation*, Dean Burgon ($25+$4 S&H) A hardback book, 610 pages in length.
[ ] Send *Summary of Inspiration* by Dr. Waite ($3 + $2 S&H)
[ ] Send *Contemporary Eng. Version Exposed*, DAW ($3+$2)
[ ] Send *Westcott & Hort's Greek Text & Theory Refuted by Burgon's Revision Revised--Summarized* by Dr. D. A. Waite ($7.00 + $3 S&H), 120 pages, perfect bound.
[ ] Send *Defending the King James Bible* by Dr.Waite $13+$4 S&H) A hardback book, indexed with study questions.
[ ] Send *Guide to Textual Criticism* by Edward Miller ($7 +$4)
[ ] Send *Westcott's Denial of Resurrection*, Dr. Waite ($4+$3)
[ ] Send *Four Reasons for Defending KJB* by DAW ($3+$3)
[ ] Send *Vindicating Mark 16:9-20* by Dr. Waite ($3+$3 S&H)
[ ] Send *Dean Burgon's Confidence in KJB* by DAW ($3+$3)
[ ] Send *Readability of A.V. (KJB)* by D. A. Waite, Jr. ($6 +$3)
[ ] Send *NIV Inclusive Language Exposed* by DAW ($5+$3)
[ ] Send *26 Hours of KJB Seminar* (4 videos) by DAW ($50.00)
[ ] Send *Defined King James Bible* lg.prt. leather ($40+$6)
[ ] Send *Defined King James Bible* med. prt. leather ($35+$5)
[ ] Send the "DBS Articles of Faith & Organization" (N.C.)
[ ] Send Brochure #1: "1000 Titles Defending KJB/TR"(N.C.)

Send or Call Orders to:
THE BIBLE FOR TODAY
900 Park Ave., Collingswood, NJ 08108
Phone: 856-854-4452; FAX:--2464; Orders: 1-800 JOHN 10:9
E-Mail Orders: BFT@BibleForToday.org; Credit Cards OK

Order Blank (p. 3)

Name:_____

Address:_____

City & State:_____ Zip:_____

Credit Card#:_____ Expires:_____

More Materials on the KJB &T.R.

[ ] Send *Summary of Traditional Text* by Dr. Waite ($3 +$2)
[ ] Send *Summary of Causes of Corruption*, DAW ($3+$2)
[ ] Send *Heresies of Westcott & Hort* by Dr. Waite ($7 + $3)
[ ] Send *Scrivener's Greek New Testament Underlying the King James Bible*, hardback, ($14 + $4 S&H)
[ ] Send *Scrivener's Annotated Greek New Testament*, by Dr. Frederick Scrivener: Hardback--($35 + $5 S&H) Genuine Leather--($45 + $5 S&H)
[ ] Send *Why Not the King James Bible?--An Answer to James White's KJVO Book* by Dr. K. D. DiVietro, ($10 + $4 S&H)
[ ] Send *Forever Settled--Bible Documents & History Survey* by Dr. Jack Moorman, ($20+$4 S&H) Hardback book.

[ ] Send *Early Church Fathers & the A.V.--A Demonstration* by Dr. Jack Moorman, ($6 + $4 S&H)
[ ] Send *When the KJB Departs from the So-Called "Majority Text"* by Dr. Jack Moorman, ($16 + $4 S&H)
[ ] Send *Missing in Modern Bibles--Nestle-Aland & NIV Errors* by Dr. Jack Moorman, ($8 + $4 S&H)
[ ] Send *The Doctrinal Heart of the Bible--Removed from Modern Versions* by Dr. Jack Moorman, VCR, ($15 +$4 S&H)
[ ] Send *Modern Bibles--The Dark Secret* by Dr. Jack Moorman, ($5 + $2 S&H)
[ ] Send *Early Manuscripts and the A.V.--A Closer* Look, by Dr. Jack Moorman, ($15 + $4 S&H)

Send or Call Orders to:
THE BIBLE FOR TODAY
900 Park Ave., Collingswood, NJ 08108
Phone: 856-854-4452; FAX:--2464; Orders: 1-800 JOHN 10:9
E-Mail Orders: BFT@BibleForToday.org; Credit Cards OK

The Defined King James Bible

UNCOMMON WORDS DEFINED ACCURATELY

I. Deluxe Genuine Leather

✦Large Print--Black or Burgundy✦
1 for $40.00+$6 S&H
✦Case of 12 for✦
$30.00 each+$30 S&H

✦Medium Print--Black or Burgundy✦
1 for $35.00+$5 S&H
✦Case of 12 for✦
$25.00 each+$24 S&H

II. Deluxe Hardback Editions

1 for $20.00+$6 S&H (Large Print)
✦Case of 12 for✦
$15.00 each+$30 S&H (Large Print)

1 for $15.00+$5 S&H (Medium Print)
✦Case of 12 for✦
$10.00 each+$24 S&H (Medium Print)

Order Phone: 1-800-JOHN 10:9